GARY E. MARTIN
14471 CR 34
Goshen, IN 46526

The Way
of the
Cross
and
Resurrection

The Way of the Cross and Resurrection

Meditations for the
Lenten Season

John M. Drescher, Editor

HERALD PRESS
Scottdale, Pennsylvania
Kitchener, Ontario
1978

Library of Congress Cataloging in Publication Data

Main entry under title:
The way of the Cross and Resurrection.

    1. Lent—Prayer-books and devotions—English.
2. Jesus Christ—Crucifixion—Meditations. 3. Jesus
Christ—Resurrection—Meditations. I. Drescher,
John M.
BV85.W37   242'.34   77-25443
ISBN 0-8361-1844-8 pbk.

THE WAY OF THE CROSS AND RESURRECTION
Copyright © 1978 by Herald Press, Scottdale, Pa. 15683
    Published simultaneously in Canada by Herald Press,
    Kitchener, Ont. N2G 4M5
Library of Congress Catalog Card Number: 77-25443
International Standard Book Number: 0-8361-1844-8
Printed in the United States of America
Design: Alice B. Shetler

10 9 8 7 6 5 4 3 2 1

To Clayton and Martha Keener,
my parents-in-law,
lifelong Christian leaders and educators
in the United States and Ethiopia.

CONTENTS

PREFACE

Soon after Christ's death His followers were called people of "The Way." They received this name not only because they professed belief in Christ but because they followed in His steps, they understood that one must live the way Christ lived.

The puspose of *The Way of the Cross and Resurrection* is expressed in the words of Hans Denck (1500-1527), "No one can truly know Christ except he follow Him in life." Many wish to take the *benefits* of the cross and resurrection while refusing to take the *way* of the cross and resurrection. The atonement cannot be separated from the Christian ethic. The resurrection cannot be detached from the Christian walk in newness of life. As Paul Erb writes in *Don't Park Here,* "A salvation, only intellectually perceived, and not permeating the whole personality is not true salvation; it may be a vicious substitute for what God has provided."

Richard C. Raines once cited the letter of a child who wrote, "Dear God, What is it like to die? Nobody will tell me. I just want to know. I don't want to do it."

Bishop Raines comments, "We tend to do that spiritually. 'Oh, God, what is it like to be converted? Nobody will tell me. I don't want to do it. I just want to know about it.' "

What a contrast this attitude is to that character with

the "strong countenance" in Bunyan's *Pilgrim's Progress*. Considering the cost of committing himself to Christ he boldly concludes, "Set my name down, sir. For I've looked the whole thing in the face, and cost me what it may, I mean to have Christlikeness and I will."

Such devotion and discipleship makes faith real and radiant. Unless we are determined to follow Christ, all our discussions are delusions. Real Christianity starts where the talk stops and the action of living begins.

Doctrine is worthless until it makes a difference in life. The purpose of revelation is transformation. Yet we persist in making discipleship a matter of muttering phrases instead of following a Person.

So Christianity is often pictured as a soft, flabby aesthetic thing that has little if anything to do with real life. So people talk about bearing the cross when they mean getting along with a cantankerous neighbor or suffering a touch of rheumatism. Jesus uses the term "cross" in referring to *all* who follow Him and the cross refers to the suffering *all* will bear who follow "in His steps."

Jacob Boehme, the mystic, once wrote: "That man is no Christian who merely comforts himself with the suffering, death, and satisfaction of Christ and who imputes it to himself as a gift or favor, while he himself remains a wild and unmanagable beast. If the sacrifice is to avail for me, it must be wrought in me."

Guido in *The Ring and the Book* says:

> I think I never was at any time
> A Christian, as you nickname all the world.

Leslie Weatherhead ponders Guido's statement and says, "I wonder if it is a nickname rather than a true description. I wonder whether Peter would recognize me as a follower of Christ in the sense in which he understood the term after the resurrection. And I wonder whether what we have produced is really Christianity at all or something quite different—not nearly as strenuous, not nearly so austere, not nearly as beautiful."

So there must be identification with the cross and the resurrection to the point that we die to the old life and walk in newness of life. We must identify with the cross in denying ourselves for the Father's will, taking up the cross, the result of that denial, and walking in resurrection life.

In these chapters each writer's approach and style is different. Some readers will appreciate one writer more than another. The unifying thread, however, that ties all the essays together is identification with Christ's cross and resurrection.

May you find spiritual enrichment from these pages and a fresh call to follow Christ. The many illustrations found here not only enliven the content and teaching but can be of much help to those preparing meditations and sermons for the Lenten season.

> John M. Drescher
> Scottdale, Pennsylvania

The Way of the Cross:
Its Benefits

John Thomstom *writes of a friend who took his exercise each Thursday by swimming in the YMCA pool. He noticed that an excellent swimmer who came to the pool each week, before he entered the water, would go to the edge of the pool, dip in his toe, like the most inexperienced swimmer, then climb to the highest diving board, make a perfect dive, and swim in top form.*

One night he asked him why he does that. The man smiled and said, "I suppose you might call it force of habit. However, there is a reason." And he told this story. He was a physical instructor at a large college. His speciality was swimming and diving. One night he had difficulty sleeping and to relax he decided to slip into the pool. Since he knew every inch, he did not turn on the lights. Besides the glass roof allowed the moon to shine in throwing his shadow on the wall.

"My body and arms made a perfect cross," he said. "I can't explain why I did not dive in that moment. But as I stood looking at the shadow of the cross, though I was not a Christian, I thought of the words of a song I learned as a child.

> *He died that we might be forgiven,*
> *He died to make us good,*
> *That we might go at last to heaven*
> *Saved by His precious blood.*

"I cannot tell you how long I stood posed on the diving board. But finally I came down. I walked along the pool to the steps and went to the bottom of the pool. I reached the bottom and my feet touched the cold, smooth bottom. The caretaker had drained the pool the day before. I knew nothing of it. I realized then, that had I dived, I would have dived to my death.

"The cross on the wall saved me that night. I was so thankful to God for His mercy in sparing my life that I knelt on the cold bricks and asked the Christ of the cross into my life. I experienced a twofold deliverance that night."

1

THE WAY OF THE CROSS: ITS BENEFITS

By John M. Drescher

For Christ also died for sins once for all, the righteous for the unrighteous, that he might bring us to God. 1 Peter 3:18.

Carroll S. Ringgold tells of a white cross which stood on the outskirts of a city. A little lad was lost in the city. A policeman inquired, "Where do you live? Just tell me where you live." But the boy did not know his address. Finally, upon further questioning, the small fellow said, "Take me to the cross on the hillside, and I can find my way home from there."

In the center of the centuries God placed a cross. And it is clear from Scripture we "must needs go home by the way of the cross. There is no other way but this." That is, we need to accept the benefits of the cross in order to come to God. The way of the cross leads home to the Father.

A writer in the *Interpreter's Bible* rightly said, any at-

John M. Drescher, Scottdale, Pennsylvania, is author of a number of books, including *Spirit Fruit, Seven Things Children Need,* and *Meditations for the Newly Married.*

tempt on the preacher's part to define the cross is like "trying to wrap a package with a piece of paper that is too small."

> For the love of God is broader
> Than the measure of man's mind.

Even though we see imperfectly and though we will never fully comprehend the cross, we see something of its meaning, and "Christ crucified" is at the center of our faith.

"If we approach the cross for *examination*," said G. Campbell Morgan, "it will evade us. If we approach it for *contemplation*, it will bewilder us. The only way to approach and understand the cross is by *identification*. That is *my* place. He died *for me* and took *my place* in His death.

"You ask me how I know God loves me," continues Morgan, "and I take you not to the infinite spaces where the stars march in splendor, nor to the garden where God smiles in flowers . . . but I point you to the bloody and brutal cross of Calvary and say, 'I know He loves me.'"

> I know not how that Calvary's cross
> A world from sin could free;
> I only know its matchless love
> Has brought God's life to me.

1. *The Way of the Cross Is the Way of Redemption*

God's grace, the Apostle Paul says, is connected with the death of Jesus Christ. To illustrate what he means he uses two very significant words, *redemption* and *expiation*. "Since all have sinned and fall short of the glory of God, they are justified by his grace as a gift, through the redemption which is in Christ Jesus, whom God put forward as an expiation by his blood, to be received by faith" (Romans 3:23-25). When he mentioned redemption, he probably was thinking of the old Hebrew custom under which a Hebrew who had become a slave was bought back out of his slavery. he was redeemed by his next of kin. Paul applies this word to the dying Christ who bought us out of the slavery of sin, paying the price with His life. "In him we have redemption through his blood."

David E. Wells points out that "The New Testament never says that Christ lived for us, thirsted for us, was tempted for us, or became weary for us, true as all this is. What it says, and says repeatedly, is that He died for us. More precisely, it says that He died for our sins, bearing them as His own, assuming responsibility for them, and suffering the full wrath of God in consequence." Sins must be suffered for.

Peter speaks also of the redemption through Christ's blood. "You know that you were ransomed from the futile ways inherited from your fathers, not with perishable things such as silver or gold, but with the precious blood of Christ, like that of a lamb without blemish or spot" (1 Peter 1:18, 19).

All through the New Testament we read that Christ's death was a sacrifice (1 Corinthians 5:7 and Ephesians 5:2, for example). This also goes back to the Old Testament, to the times when a lamb was offered up on the altar as an expiation or sacrifice. The man knew he deserved death for his sin but God allowed him to offer up the innocent lamb as a substitute.

Years ago there was a play on Broadway called "Green Pastures." One of the scenes portrayed God looking down upon the earth while talking with Gabriel. God asked, "What more can I do to deliver them?"

Then a shadow fell across the stage and Gabriel inquired, "Who's shadow is that?"

"That's Hosea's shadow," God replied.

"Does that mean," Gabriel asked, "that as Hosea suffered to redeem his wayward wife, so God suffers to redeem His people?"

"Yes," God answered, "that's what it means."

As they continued looking down they saw a man carrying a cross. But it wasn't His own cross. he carried it for another. He was taking the place of the one who deserved to die. The cross is the price paid to redeem us, to deliver us, to set us free from sin.

> Was it for crimes that I have done
> He groaned upon the tree?
> Amazing pity! Grace unknown!
> And love beyond degree!

Through the cross we are redeemed from the curse of the law we have broken (Galatians 3:13). Through the cross we are redeemed from the bondage, the power, and the practice of sin.

> He breaks the power of canceled sin,
> He sets the prisoner free;
> His blood can wash the foulest clean,
> His blood availed for me.

God through the cross "has delivered us from the dominion of darkness and transferred us to the kingdom of his beloved Son, in whom we have redemption, the forgiveness of sins" (Colossians 1:13, 14).

Guenter Rutenborn in his play, *The Signs of Jonah,*

growing out of the suffering and brutality of World War II, describes a unique trial. A cross-section of humanity is the jury—represented by a mother, a man on the street, a merchant, and a queen. Each in his own way has been a victim of the evil forces in the world. Each is seeking for a way out of his feeling of guilt, casting about for someone to blame.

Argument after argument finally leads the jury to shout out in unison, "God is guilty!" Then the jury begins to mete out sentences against God, collecting evidence from the worst of their own sufferings and finally producing the following verdict: "God Himself must become a man. He must be thrust out from the highest of His kingly honors. He must face the filth and insults of others and be forced to wear a crown of thorns. He must wander in the earth without rights, without home, hungry and thirsty, knowing the terror of death. The misery of the people must press upon Him day and night. The maimed and the leprous shall surround Him. He must look at stinking corpses. He must know the pain of what it means to lose an only son. At last let Him sink to His knees with the sweat breaking out of Him like drops of blood under the curse of being a man, and then let Him die, dishonored and ridiculed."

As the sentence is handed down it begins to dawn upon the audience with great clarity that God already has paid the penalty. Although he was not on trial He paid the penalty anyway. "God so loved the world that he gave his only Son, that whoever believes in him should not perish but have eternal life."

This is what Calvary means—Christ took our place. He paid the price so we could be redeemed, bought back. He suffered for us.

In the cross we see God's love for us. "By this we know love, that he laid down his life for us" (1 John 3:16). Divine love is not ever understood outside the context of the cross. If you want the uttermost proof of love you must go to the cross.

> There on the cross 'tis fairest drawn,
> In precious blood and crimson lines.

Love is measured by the length it will go in the way of sacrifice. "Greater love has no man than this," said Jesus, "that a man lay down his life for his friends." *A Tale of Two Cities* we are told stands alone among the works of Dickens in dignity and eloquence. That great and moving story culminates in the sacrifice of Sidney Carton, who went to the guillotine to save the life of the husband of the lady he also loved. Life was pleasant to him and death bitter. But for love he died, a love he had given expression to many times in his life but now supremely in his death.

And so it is with Christ's love. All through His life He gave expression to His love in beautiful words and gracious deeds. But if you want to see Christ's love you must see Him die. He died for love. It was not the high priests and Pilate who put Him to death. He laid down His life voluntarily.

But the love of Christ was a mightier love than the love of Sidney Carton. Carton died for a friend. Christ died, the just for the unjust, to bring us to God.

As a result of that redemption we now love Him. And we are enabled to love others whom He loves. A sign that we have been redeemed is that we desire to see others redeemed. A sign that we have been forgiven is that now we find it possible to forgive. A sign that we have accepted Christ's love is that now we practice redemptive love toward others.

Christianity is the gospel of redemption.

2. *The Way of the Cross Is the Way of Reconciliation*

Reconciliation takes place in the area of relationships. Individuals or groups that were enemies find a common ground and can live at peace with each other. Being reconciled means not only that we are justified or freed from our own just guilt and punishment, but we now can experience a new life together. Reconciliation brings together those who were separated. Former enemies are now at peace. The cross of Christ put an end to the separation which existed and replaced alienation with peace and fellowship.

The Apostle Paul describes the next step of reconciliation in Romans 5:8-11. "But God shows his love for us in that while we were yet sinners Christ died for us. Since, therefore, we are now justified by his blood, much more shall we be saved by him from the wrath of God. For if while we were enemies we were reconciled to God by the death of his Son, much more, now that we are reconciled, shall we be saved by his life. Not only so, but we also rejoice in God through our Lord Jesus Christ, through whom we have now received our reconciliation."

Also in Ephesians 2:13, 14 reconciliation is described with beauty and clarity. "But now in Christ Jesus you who once were far off have been brought near in the blood of Christ. For he is our peace, who has made us both one, and has broken down the dividing wall of hostility."

The reconciling work through the cross is carried on in three great areas or spheres.

(a) *Through the cross we are reconciled with God.*
The fact that unregenerate persons are strangers to God
and alienated from God is axiomatic in the Scripture and
all life bears it out. Separation from God is the result of
two things—ignorance and sin. One might say that ignorance itself is the result of sin.

Through sin man has become ignorant of what kind of
God He really is. The god of this world has blinded the
eyes of those who believe not. To such God is a harsh,
cruel, vengeful being. The true God which Christ
brought to us, on the other hand, is a God whose very
character is love. He is a compassionate, searching God
who is always longing to save and help and give His best
for each person. We see on the cross what God is like and
how far God will go to save us. The cross demonstrates
what is repeatedly stated in the Scripture—God loves us
and wants us to love Him in return. The cross clears the
character of God which was not understood through the
ignorance brought on by sin. And then one day God, in
His Son, climbed a cruel cross, opened His arms to all
man's meanness and madness and said, "If this is what it
takes to bring man back again, I'll do it." Yes, in the cross
we see the kind of God we have—a God altogether dif-
erent from the kind of God which separated man
imagines.

We were separated from God by sin. The immediate
effect of sin in the Garden of Eden was fear and estrangement. Adam and Eve hid themselves. As Isaiah solemnly
put it, "Your iniquities have made a separation between
you and your God." The Apostle Paul says we were
separated, alienated by our wicked works, and strangers
to God's promises through sin. In Colossians he adds that
we were enemies in our minds. That is what sin does. A

person with sin in the soul seeks to evade God, to resist His Spirit, and reacts against the claims of God.

So the very core of the gospel is that Christ, through the cross, reconciles us to God. By His seeking, stooping, sacrificial love we can again have peace with God. He wrought peace through His cross. The cross says the sentence of condemnation is no longer against us and if we accept it we are at peace with God.

(b) *Through the cross we are reconciled between ourselves and our consciences.* Sin does more than create a breech between God and us. It creates a guilty conscience—a breech between us and our better selves. This is the reason "there is no peace to the wicked." This is not a threat but a spiritual law. The sinner sins against his better self. "Duncan hath murdered sleep," moaned Macbeth—though it was not Duncan but his sin heavy on his conscience which killed sleep.

Once again Jesus mediates peace. Through the cross He blots out our sin. "He gives the guilty conscience peace." Through His blood our "hearts sprinkled clean from an evil conscience."

(c) *Through the cross we are reconciled with others.* Barriers, walls, partitions which separate are broken down through the cross. When we experience Christ's love, when we are reconciled to God and others, the enmity between us and others must go. In fact He gave us the ministry of reconciliation. "All this is from God, who through Christ reconciled us to himself and gave us the ministry of reconciliation; that is, God was in Christ reconciling the world to himself, not counting their trespasses against them,and entrusting to us the message of reconciliation. So we are ambassadors for Christ, God making his appeal through us. We beseech you on behalf of Christ, be reconciled to God" (2 Corinthians 5:18-20).

When the love of Christ is shed abroad in our hearts, the warfare ceases.

Redemption's result is *love* for God and others. The result of reconciliation is that we have peace with God, ourselves, and others. Christianity is the gospel of reconciliation.

3. *The Way of the Cross Is the Way of Restoration.*

Not only does Christ, through the cross, redeem us and reconcile us but He also restores us to the place we would have if we had never sinned. What we lost through the fall is restored through Christ. George Rawson wrote a common hymn in the middle of the nineteenth century:

> By Christ redeemed, in Christ restored,
> We keep the memory adored,
> And show the death of our dear Lord
> Until He come.

The redeeming, reconciling, and restoring Christian faith is in the cross. Nothing has the power to cleanse, purge, and restore but the cross. It is at the cross—like Bunyan's Christian—that we lose our burdens and sins and find restoring grace. Remove the cross or reduce it to a mere ethic and it is useless to restore the sinner.

(a) *The approval of God is again restored.* Through sin we lost God's approval. We did not lose His love.

We are justified by faith. God, through Christ, accepts and approves us. "There is therefore now no condemnation for those who are in Christ Jesus" (Romans 8:1). The believer is made secure against all condemnation by the death, resurrection, ascension, and intercession of Christ. The whole past account is wiped out.

> My sin! O the bliss of this glorious thought!
> My sin! not in part, but the whole,
> Is nailed to the cross and I bear it no more;
> Praise the Lord, praise the Lord, O my soul!

So complete is that restoration that we are called God's own children. "Beloved, we are God's children now" (1 John 3:2). Jesus said, "I in them and thou in me, that they may become perfectly one, so that the world may know that thou hast sent me and hast loved them even as thou hast loved me."

An unknown poet wrote:

> Near, so very near to God,
> Nearer I cannot be.
> For in the person of His Son
> I'm just as near as He.

> Dear, so very very dear to God.
> Dearer I cannot be;
> For in the person of His Son
> I'm just as dear as He.

(b) *The nature of God is again restored.* Through our sin we lost the nature of God and became the children of wrath. We became like our father the devil and were obedient to him. But now through the cross we have received the divine nature.

As Augustine so aptly observed, the divine became human so that the human might become divine. Christ shared our lot so that we might share His. This is how our salvation was accomplished.

This is what being a Christian means, according to the New Testament—sharing in the very life of Christ. It is no mere external imitation of Christ but rather allowing Christ Himself to live again in us. We sing:

Thy nature, gracious Lord, impart;
Come quickly from above.

This means partaking of Christ's nature. The *imitatio Christe* may be nothing more than a more exacting and burdensome legalism. The phrase in 2 Peter 1:4, "partakers of the divine nature," means we are changed at the very core and center of our being.

A photographer had an old daguerreotype brought to him for possible restoration. The image had become so faded and corroded that one could not distinguish the features. He took the apparently useless likeness into his workroom, poured over it a certain solution, then subjected it to intense heat, and the image was restored. A face of beauty and sweetness replaced the blurred picture.

If an earthly photographer can restore a likeness that seems hopelessly lost, how much more surely can the One who made us restore the soul, blurred and marred by sin, into the image and likeness of God.

(c) *The knowledge of God is restored.* Through sin we lose the knowledge of God. Sin blinds our eyes. Sin keeps us from seeing or understanding God. The pure in heart see God now and hereafter. And through the cross we are again purified by faith. The Holy Spirit reveals Christ to us and in revealing Christ to us shows us our God of love. We never really know God, or understand His love, until we come to know Him through the cross. Here His love is displayed. Here His real character is demonstrated. "By this we know love, that he laid down his life for us." "For," says Paul, "if while we were enemies we were reconciled to God by the death of his Son, much more, now that we are reconciled, shall we be saved by his life."

(d) *Fellowship with God is again restored.* Sin breaks fellowship. Sin shuts us out from God's presence. Now through the cross we have access again to God. The veil is rent. We come to Him through the new and living way which is Christ Himself. "And our fellowship is with the Father and with his Son Jesus Christ."

So it is that by the power of the cross all who believe are united with Him in the fellowship of His death and in the fellowship of His resurrection. In a world where many souls are yearning for peace, let the church of Jesus Christ fearlessly and faithfully preach the gospel of the cross of Christ. Only as the fellowship with sin is broken in the hearts of persons can they come to living fellowship with God. Not until the barrier of sin is removed, can union with God in Christ be restored. And apart from fellowship in His death and resurrection spiritual brotherhood exists only in name.

Through the cross we experience a restoration.

> Down in the human heart, crushed by the tempter,
> Feelings lie buried that grace can restore;
> Touched by a loving hand, wakened by kindness,
> Chords that are broken will vibrate once more.

The result of restoration is hope. And the hope of the Christian is not a wish but an assured conviction of what will yet take place in all its fullness. We, who were without hope and without God in the world, have a living, lasting hope through the cross. Christianity is the gospel of restoration.

"The cross," says William Barclay, "is proof that there is no length to which the love of God will refuse to go to

win men's hearts. The cross is the medium of reconciliation because the cross is the final proof of the love of
God, and a love like that demands an answering love."

The Way of the Cross:
Its Implications

We can put a cross on top of a church building or hang it on the wall of our home, we can wear it as an ornament around the neck, we can place a cross as a bookmark in the Bible. But it is quite another thing to let the cross of Christ make accursed everything in that old life, until it is impossible for us, knowingly and wilfully to give the devil place, or to be conformed to the world in any part of our life or to allow self still to have sovereignty over us.

—Ruth Paxson in *Called unto Holiness* (Moody Press)

We can carry the cross on high banners, preach the cross, sing of its wondrous power until we are hoarse. But it will accomplish little unless the marks of the crucifixion appear in the suffering, the denial, the scorn, the unpopularity we are willing to undergo on behalf of persons. When we Christians are concerned enough to die a little for the sake of persons for whom Christ died, then perhaps we only begin to be evangelists who are worthy of the Christ we serve.

So it is meaningless to hear a stranger say, "God loves you," if no accompanying evidence, someone here and now, someone who cares enough to risk a little on your behalf says, "I love you." Real love must become incarnate in persons rather than in pronouncements and programs.—Kenneth Morse

2

THE WAY OF THE CROSS:
ITS IMPLICATIONS

By John M. Drescher

Anyone who does not take his cross and follow in my foot-steps is not worthy of me. Matthew 10:38, Jerusalem Bible.

Jacob Enz, professor of Old Testament at Associated Biblical Seminaries, Elkhart, Indiana, wrote an article, "The Biblical Imperative for Discipleship." In it he presents a theology which links together inseparably word and work, profession and discipleship. In strong words Dr. Enz writes, "The colossal error of modern Christianity is to welcome with open arms all the precious benefits of the blood of Christ so freely poured out for us and then, sometimes ignorantly, often studiously, and sometimes even defiantly, to reject the method by which redemption was wrought out—living self-sacrificing love to the bitter end and beyond. . . . We embrace the cross Christ bore for us and fling from us as a red-hot

John M. Drescher, Scottdale, Pennsylvania, is author of a number of books, including *Follow Me, Now Is the Time to Love,* and *Talking It Over.*

iron the cross He gives us to bear!''

Professor Enz goes on to say that in doing this we stand in the unholy tradition of Peter who at one moment, as the rock, confesses the Christ and the next moment crumbles into the sands of demonic instability as he seeks to keep Christ from going the way of the cross. "We still want the glory but not the scandal of Christ!"

Some years ago *Time* magazine recorded the observations made by a large ecumenical group meeting in Boston. "When we consider how little it costs to be counted among church members in our country today, we are troubled. The average church member is not conspicuously different from the nonmember. The average church is so conformed to the world that people are surprised if it sharply challenges the prevailing behavior of the community."

Dietrich Bonhoeffer in his challenging volume, *The Cost of Discipleship,* calls this kind of Christianity "cheap grace." It is grace without a cross, grace without a living Lord, grace without discipleship. It is not Christian grace. A disciple of Christ, on the other hand, is a learner of Jesus and learning, lives in the same spirit as Jesus. A disciple is one who walks in the way of Christ which means he takes the way of the cross of Christ as his way also.

Christ Asks for a Verdict

This is exactly what Jesus says in Matthew 16:24, "If any man would come after me, let him deny himself and take up his cross and follow me." To follow Christ is to take the same path He has taken. And there is no exception, for He says, "If *any* man," meaning of course any person, man or woman.

Looking into the context of these words in Matthew we see Jesus was in *danger*. It was the first time the Pharisees and Sadducees, the religious power groups, combined to destroy Him. It was a time of *discouragement*. Matthew describes the dullness of the disciples after nearly three years under Jesus' teaching. It was a time of *doubt* on the part of His followers. Many who had followed Him now left Him.

We are told that Jesus brought His twelve faithful disciples to Caesarea Philippi to probe their understanding of who He was, their loyalty, and whether they would continue to follow Him.

Scattered around the area were the temples of Baal worship, fourteen in the immediate vicinity. Jesus and His disciples met in the shadow of the ancient gods. Nearby was the hill and cave said to be the birthplace of the great god Pam. Legend said all the gods gathered at Caesarea Philippi. Here was the great temple of white marble built to the godhead of Caesar and within sight where Israel had worshiped the golden calf.

This was the place Jesus brought His disciples. What a dramatic picture—a penniless Galilean carpenter and twelve ordinary men. All the orthodox people of the time were trying to eliminate Him, considering Him a dangerous heretic. All around were the temples of the gods. Against the background of the world's gods and religions Jesus asked for a verdict as to who He was.

Numerous answers were given by the onlookers. "John the Baptist," some said. That was Herod's terrified opinion. Jesus was a kind of ghost sent to haunt him for murdering John the Baptist. "Elias," said others—a reformer, taken up without dying whom Malachi said would return again. "Jeremiah" still others suggested, for some thought according to 2 Maccabees 2 he would return and reveal the place of the tabernacle, ark, and altar of incense. Some suggested He was "one of the prophets," like a celebrated sage of the past.

The responses show that Jesus was held in high reputation by some. But they indicate that few, if any, regarded Him as the Messiah.

Then Jesus turned to His chosen twelve and asked for their opinion. They had lived with Him, observed His life, and knew that it conformed to what He had taught. They had seen His miracles and heard His claims. While many had left when His demands seemed too difficult, these disciples did not desert Him. What did they really think of Him?

Peter came through strongly. He said, "You are the Christ, the Son of the living God." And Jesus said that was no human revelation. God had revealed to Peter who He really was. "And," said Jesus, "I will build my church, and the powers of death shall not prevail against it." This is the first time the word *church* is used in the New Testament.

Against all this background Jesus now spoke of the divine necessity of the cross. Long before this time His purpose was clear to Him. Even though His disciples did not yet understand the idea of a suffering Messiah which Isaiah so clearly prophesied, Jesus knew He had come to die. Peter tried to steer Him from the cross. But Jesus knew this was the same sort of temptation He suffered from Satan in the wilderness. He would have none of it.

Notice then in Matthew 16:21-27 three statements concerning the path of Jesus, three corresponding statements concerning the path of His disciples, and three great incentives which flow from the former.

1. The Path of Jesus

(a) "*I must go to Jerusalem.*" Here is the "must" of the Father's will. "Why must Christ go?" Because it was the Father's will for Him! It is the same "must" which He spoke of at the age of twelve: "I must be in my Father's house." Later in Luke 4:43 He said, "I must preach the good news of the kingdom of God." So also in John 4:4 He said, "I must go through Samaria." It was the complete denial of self for the Father's will. "We must work the works of him who sent me" (John 9:4). The climate of Christ's life was continual obedience in doing the will of God who sent Him. Now He *must* go to Jerusalem. Why? Because He knew it was the Father's will. His path was the Father's will. There is only one explanation for the continual use of the word "must" in the life of Jesus. It is that His desire to fulfill God's will moved Him always to take the path God wanted for Him.

(b) *I must suffer and be killed.* The cross was ahead. To suffer, to be rejected, and to be killed was Christ's path. He came for this purpose. If man is to have life, He must die. The consequence of following God and fulfilling God's will is the cross and Jesus would not evade it.

There are times when we find it easy to obey. When God calls us to green pastures and by still waters we find it easy to listen. But what about the times He summons us to climb the "steep ascent" or to tread some via dolorosa? Then, like Christ, we find the devil seeks to persuade us to take an easier way, to avoid the cross. The will of God led Christ to a painful cross.

> Privations, sorrows, bitter scorn,
> The life of toil, the mean abode,

The faithless kiss, the crown of thorns—
These were the consecrated road.

(c) *I must rise again.* This also is the path of Jesus. Resurrection follows death. The crown follows the cross. Glory follows rejection. Jesus not only predicts His death but also His resurrection. Here is the pattern—denial, death, and deliverance. This is the path of Jesus.

2. *The Path of the Disciple*

(a) *We must deny ourselves.* The path of Jesus' disciple is the same as His own path. "If any man would come after me, let him deny himself." Notice that word *if*. Jesus leaves us free to accept. We choose to be His disciples. And here in "self-denial" is the first challenge to discipleship. It's the basic one. This demands more than denying something for oneself. For us, like Christ, this means a personal, willing, and complete surrender to God over our own will, body, affections, and aspirations. It is more than merely disciplining our tastes, impulses, or desires. It is more than denying ourselves little things during Lent or other special times. It is the self-renunciation of putting God's will first in all of life.

Commentator Lange writes: "Self-renunciation of the believer is the soul of the confession of Christ. Without this the confession of Christ as Savior is meaningless." This daily denial, this giving of one's self-interests is a greater test of discipleship than dying the death of a martyr.

Medieval saints spoke of the mortification of self. That's what this denial means. If we are to say "yes" to Christ we must be willing to say "no" to self at any point we know His will conflicts with ours. J. B. Phillips says it means to "give up all rights to yourself." It has been said that the cross is simply I crossed out and so it is, "No I but Christ." As self-concern is the first law of nature so self-denial is the first law of grace.

In *The Cost of Discipleship*, Bonhoeffer writes, "No one should be surprised at the difficulty of faith, if there is some part of his life where he is consciously resisting or disobeying the commandment of Jesus. Is there some part of your life which you are refusing to surrender to His behest, some hope, perhaps your ambition or your reason? If so, you must not be surprised that you have not received the Holy Spirit, that prayer is difficult, or that your request for faith remains unanswered."

An aged saint sat with her Bible before her. "What are you doing?" a friend asked.

"I'm learning the Lord's Prayer," the godly woman answered.

"Learning the Lord's Prayer? But you learned that as a child long ago. Nearly everyone knows the Lord's Prayer."

"No, I never fully learned it. I'm still trying to learn more fully the meaning of the third phrase. 'Thy will be done.' "

In Luke 9 Jesus was confronted with three would-be disciples. One said, "I will follow you." Jesus said, "First count the cost." Mark says he was a scribe. Certainly it would be nice to have a doctor of theology on His team. But Jesus knew the man wasn't ready to give up his will to follow. He was the kind of fellow who could sing, "'Take my life and let it be.' Don't make demands. I'll follow but at the level of commitment I choose." Jesus would not accept such a man for a disciple.

A second would-be disciple when approached about

following said, "I'll follow You after my father dies. Let me go first and bury him." But Jesus cannot have a disciple with divided loyalties. Beware of letting anyone or anything interfere with complete loyalty to Him. Elsewhere He says if we love father or mother more than Him we are not worthy of Him.

A third would-be disciple promised to follow if the Lord allowed him to return first and say good-bye to the old gang. Now it's all right to say good-bye. But more was involved. Jesus knew that the home gang was smug, sedate, and content to compromise with the world. He could hear them say, "Don't get excited about this religion. It's okay to be religious but don't become radical." Christ cannot accept such a disciple.

For the first the price was too high. It meant the complete denial of self. For the second the separation was too extreme. It meant giving first loyalty to Jesus. For the third the discipleship was too confining. It meant a radical break with the past, the world, and its concerns. To all the problem was really self-denial.

(b) *We must take up our cross.* "If any man would come after me, let him deny himself and take up his cross." The cross was the result of Christ following the Father's will. So also for us. It can be avoided. The *if* is again conditional. But when that denial is really made, the cross will surely follow. Only when we become completely dead to self are we ready to bear the cross, the consequences of that denial. The cross is not a burden or hurt which saint and sinner suffer alike. It is the result of exclusive allegiance to Jesus Christ. It is the suffering or even death we are called upon to endure *because* we follow Christ.

So the cross is not having a disease or affliction to bear. It is not having to live with fewer natural possessions or natural comforts. It is not experiencing some personal misfortune. Nor does the cross speak of something that is unavoidable. It is something we *take up*. We could avoid it but we don't.

Jesus had many burdens but he never confused these with the cross. Jesus knew that the cross was the natural result of denying Himself for the Father's will.

And we will not need to look for the cross if we are following Christ. The world did not love Christ. It does not love His disciple. The world persecuted Christ. His followers cannot expect less. Jesus said every Christian had a cross waiting for him. When we start out we abandon ourselves to whatever suffering may result from following Christ, Jesus said, "Deny yourself for my will and be prepared to suffer, to be rejected, and to face the firing squad."

W. E. Sangster, in his book *Can I Know God?* writes, "There is a reproach on the gospel—even in a nominally Christian land. There is a shame at the heart of the cross, and it must be borne. You cannot have the beautiful friendship of the world and the saving friendship of Christ. . . . There is a choice to be made. And if you are going to be definite in discipleship, it must be faced; this or that, right or wrong, Christ or mammon."

Sangster goes on to say that there is "social ostracism which Christians often suffer" because they follow Christ. If we at times have not felt this, it is likely we are not following. He says sometimes a person "suffers in his professional advancement because he has identified himself with the Christian cause. Sometimes Christians are actually made a joke, a butt, an object of common contumely [scornful abuse], because they were in this way of life." How often Christians have been called mad, fanatical, off base because they follow Christ.

Sangster writes, "Not all Christians of course are suspected of madness, and it is no compliment that the dark suspicion doesn't fall. Often it means that their lives are so tepid, so lacking in challenge, so wanting in the penetrating power of holiness and the arrestings of grace that they are not conspicious in society and could pass for a pagan anywhere."

The Apostle Paul wrote, "For while we live we are always being given up to death for Jesus' sake, so that the life of Jesus may be manifested in our mortal flesh" (2 Cor. 4:11). Previously, before we experienced the work of the cross, we saw everything "for our sake." Now we interpret life for Jesus' sake. We have not been delivered from the world as long as we continue to interpret Calvary as it will benefit us, even though we may share its benefits with those who are lost, wander in our own way and preserve our own right to rule.

Keith Falconer attempted a different work for Christ in his mission among Muslims. He died in Arabia and among his few belongings were these words.

> Let people call you eccentric (because you are doing the will of God). Eccentric means nothing more than out of center, and if you have got a new center in God, of course you are out of the center of the world. Let the world's .marching move around the old center. You have begun to move about quite another pivot than that around which the world moves.

(c) *We must follow Him in resurrection life*. Paul the apostle, is quite clear. We who have died with Him in the baptism of His denial and death are risen with Him to new life. Only when there is first that denial and death can one experience the fullness of joy that the apostle knew when he triumphantly declared, "I have been crucified with Christ; it is no longer I who live, but Christ who lives in me; and the life I now live in the flesh I live by faith in the Son of God, who loved me and gave himself for me" (Galatians 2:20). This too is the way of discipleship. There is no shortcut. The pattern is clear. The way to life is through death. And the reason many know so little of the joy of Christ's life is that they are unwilling to deny themselves for His will or die to themselves.

3. *Three Corresponding Incentives*

Now Jesus gives three great incentives which seem paradoxical.

(a) *"Whoever would save his life will lose it."* This speaks to the denial of self. If you refuse to deny yourself for Christ's will, you are the loser in the end. This is illustrated all through life. In society persons grasp at life yet fail in finding it. When we do with life what we wish, it issues in that which we do not want. The most important thing in life is not the finding of freedom but the finding of a master. One does not live until one surrenders without reservation to a cause greater than oneself. So at the very threshold of His kingdom Jesus meets us and says, "If any man would come after me, let him deny himself. . . . For whoever would save his life will lose it."

The fact is that real happiness is the inevitable result of a certain kind of life. If you don't believe it search out the frustrated multitude and see how they spend their time. You will find their lives filled with desires for beaches, banquets, and belongings. Then search out the radiant few and you will find them losing themselves, sitting by sickbeds, carrying food to the hungry, standing behind pulpits, and serving others as Christ did. Dorcas with her needle will be immortal when Napoleon is forgotten. Mary with her alabaster box will live on when Alexander's name is burned in oblivion. The cup of cold water lifted in Christ's name to the lips of a lisping child will count for eternity while the great act done for self dies at the doing.

An elderly missionary, speaking to a group of seminary students said, "If you wish to be supremely happy, risk it all! If you play it safe you will be perfectly miserable." This is a central concept of the gospel and true to experience. The value of life lies in the way it is spent, not in the way it is saved.

(b) *"For what will it profit a man, if he gains the whole world and forfeits his life?"* Here is one who questions whether taking the way of the cross is worth all the suffering and perhaps even death. He decides he will not take the cross. He gains instead the applause of man. He sells his soul for the things of time. The world stands for material things and the applause of persons.

"Suppose a person is so successful that he gains the wealth of the whole world yet in the process he loses his own soul, what has he gained?" Jesus asks. Suppose you refuse to take up the cross and, instead, you gain the applause of everyone. Yet if you lose your very soul in the process, what have you accomplished?" The answer is apparent not only to human logic but also to anyone who will look at those who lose their souls in striving for material and earthly success. These things are not lasting or satisfying. And further no one can exchange such things for life. Money, lip service, nor anything else will be able to give you life or save your soul. Only the surrendered life to Christ provides salvation and ultimate satisfaction.

A third incentive to discipleship Jesus gives in this way:

(c) *"For the Son of man is to come with his angels in the glory of his Father, and then he will repay every man for what he has done."* The Lord is coming. Those who are His followers will be rewarded at His coming.

Rita Snowden, a famous writer of children's stories and books, tells of two workmen who were discussing the death of Dick Sheppard, a famous London preacher, who was a great disciple of Christ and friend of people. He died too young from a human point of view.

"Poor Dick Sheppard died," said the first.

"None of your *poor* Dick Sheppard," said the other. "God will be real glad to have him."

Here there is first a warning. Life will be judged. There will be a day of reckoning. Then there is a promise. The cross is not the end. The shame which following Christ may bring is not the end. Death is not the end. After the cross comes the crown. Christ will not forget to reward those who are His followers. Those who put Christ first, who have suffered with and for Him, and those who are raised to a new and different life through Him shall triumph with Him. And He, the loving Lord, will do the rewarding.

Charles Sheldon, in the Christian classic *In His Steps*, tells the dramatic story of how the first church of Raymond learned what it meant to follow Christ. The church had always acknowledged that it was part of their doctrine to follow Christ. But members had no idea that it should commit them to a definite lifestyle which de-manded something of them. They felt that their purpose for existing rested in what was already accomplished. They had a beautiful church. The membership was made up of the town's finest citizens. The pastor fulfilled their duty to society by presenting the challenge of the gospel Sunday after Sunday.

During the worship service one particular Sunday the soloist sang "Where He Leads Me I Will Follow." Then the pastor preached on following Christ. He discussed how Christ had redeemed men by sacrificing His life and then he outlined the steps the congregation needed to take to follow Christ's sacrifice and example.

The self-confident congregation had no intention of taking those steps and wouldn't have, had the service concluded as it usually did. But suddenly from the rear of the auditorium a ragged, unshaven man walked to the front of the church. Turning to the congregation he asked, "What do you mean when you sing, 'I'll go with Him, with Him all the way? . . . I heard you sing, 'All for Jesus, all for Jesus,' too. It seems to me there's an awful lot of trouble in the world that somehow wouldn't exist if all the people who sang such songs went and lived them out."

Among the soldiers of Alexander the Great was a young, shiftless, careless soldier by the name of Alexander. One day Alexander the Great approached this soldier whose conduct was not a compliment in his army. "What is your name?" he asked.

"Alexander," the youth replied."

In louder voice Alexander the Great asked, "What is your *name?*"

Again the soldier answered distinctly, "Alexander, your honor."

Now the General shouted, "*What is your name?*"

The young man trembling answered, "My name, sir, is Alexander."

"Then," said, Alexander the Great, "either you change your conduct or you change your name!"

If we desire to be called Christian our conduct must conform to Christ. This is the implication of the cross. The New Testament uses "disciple" as the normal name for a follower of Christ. The basic question is not "Am I a Christian?" but "Am I a disciple?" In the Great Commission Christ sends His followers out to make not just converts, but disciples.

Our King for
Every Day

He-They-We

They hailed Him King as He passed by,
They strewed their garments in the road,
But they were set on earthly things,
And He on God.

They sang His praise for that He did
But gave His message little thought;
They could not see that their souls' good
Was all He sought.

They could not understand why He,
With powers so vast at His command,
Should hesitate to claim their rights
And free the land.

Their own concerns and this world's hopes
Shut out the wonder of His news;
And we, with larger knowledge, still
His way refuse.

He walks among us still, unseen,
And still points out the only way,
But we still follow other gods
And Him betray.

—John Oxenham

3

OUR KING FOR EVERY DAY

By Bernie Wiebe

Blessed is the kingdom of our father David that is coming!
Hosanna in the highest! Mark 11:10. (See also Matthew 21:1-
11, Mark 11:1-11. Luke 19:28-44, and John 12:12-19.)

On Thursday, November 21, 1963, President John F. Kennedy and his wife, Jacqueline, flew to Texas. They went there to build up shaky political relationships. Receptions at San Antonio, Houston, and Fort Worth were accepting and enthusiastic. Everything was going better than their highest expectations.

On Friday, November 22, at 11:37 a.m. the big presidential jet, *Air Force One*, landed at Dallas. The city's greeting, like the 76-degree temperature, was warm and refreshing. The presidential motorcade left the airport at 11:50. At 12:30 p.m., three shots rang out within six seconds. At 1:33 p.m., John F. Kennedy was declared dead at Parkland Memorial Hospital in Dallas.

Bernie Wiebe, Winnipeg, Manitoba, has worked in radio and television productions, is past president of Freeman Junior College and Freeman Academy in North Dakota, and presently edits *The Mennonite*

What began as an exciting new page in the Kennedy affair with Texas became one of the darkest pages in United States history. The turn of events shocked the whole world and left many people wondering to this day how such a thing is humanly possible.

One of the early television game shows was called *Queen for a Day*. Out of the many contestants, one lucky person emerged as the big winner. A lifetime of waiting and dreaming was suddenly fulfilled. She was given almost anything her heart and mind could desire—*for one day*. She literally became a pampered queen for twenty-four hours.

Both illustrations relate directly to Palm Sunday.

1. The Messianic Hope

People of the Western world have relatively short histories and memories. Long ago, at most, may mean two centuries of the United States and barely 110 years for Canada. That's when our countries were born.

It wasn't so with the Jews in Jesus' day. Some of the people had lived on the same piece of family land for thousands of years. They traced their ancestry back to Abraham and the promise to become "a great nation" (Genesis 12:2a). Moses and Joshua carried on that promise. God assured their beloved King David that his descendants would sit on the throne forever (2 Samuel 7:8-29). This divine commitment from a covenant God became an undying hope.

Of course, as humans are prone to do, the people built on the idyllic. Internal problems were overlooked; external oppressors were regarded as temporary. The messianic hope became focused—they would see a new and perfect king, a shoot from the stock of Jesse would come to reign as the Wonderful Counselor, Mighty God, Everlasting Father, and Prince of Peace (Isaiah 2:1-4; 9:2-7; 11:1-9; Amos 9:11; Jeremiah 33:14-22; Ezekiel 37:24-28).

It was a terrible shock when this idyllic future was delayed by the Babylonian exile and some of the bitter religious rivalries which developed among their own religious leaders.

The signs seemed to be for better times once again when the temple was restored and the Torah (God's law) once more came to be the guide under Ezra and others of the priests.

But then came the shattering blow of Palestine's takeover by the Seleucids and the infamous decrees of Antiochus Epiphanes (168 BC) aimed at destroying the religion of Israel and demanding worship of the Greek gods by the Jews.

Some now felt that God would want them to usher in the messianic age by their own hands. Zealots organized terrorist activity to overthrow the foreign tyrants and to establish an egalitarian society.

Others felt that this was the ultimate test of their faithfulness. They must have faith in God's power to save and be ready to die rather than to violate His law.

Still others began to spiritualize their messianic hope. They would yet see the new kingdom but it would be a heavenly one.

And there were many who held on to the prophetic hope, assigning the prophetic vision now to a prophetlike figure who would arise in their midst and establish a new Jerusalem with a powerful Davidic empire. For them, the glorious messianic hope was as real and powerful as it could possibly be.

2. *The Prelude*

In this climate of confusion and messianic reassessment by some, Jesus was born. His early history is sometimes called the "hidden years" because the Gospels tell us so little about his first thirty years. Luke tells of Jesus' going to the temple in Jerusalem at age twelve. We are told that He lived with His family at Nazareth and on the Sabbath he attended services (Luke 4:16). We know that His father, Joseph, was a carpenter and it appears that Jesus followed His father's vocation until He was about thirty. From His parables, it is clear that He was an astute observer of human behavior.

The first sign of any real action gets underway when John the Baptist, a fiery orator, begins to attract large crowds with a preaching that bluntly called people to repent because the day of judgment was at hand. He warned people against relying on ancestry or privilege; only a personal repentance and commitment to new life through baptism would show the world whose followers they really were.

Jesus Himself boldly stepped before John, requested baptism, and then ventured forth from the Jordan into the wilderness. There He wrestled with the same messianic hopes and temptations that His fellow Jews had faced over the years.

In this person-to-person encounter with Satan, Jesus clearly perceived Himself to be the Messiah on God's terms alone.

For three years Jesus preached, taught a small band of disciples, performed miracles, and healed the needy.

Those whose minds envisioned a different Messiah regarded Jesus as an intruder, a blasphemer, and a playboy. Their opposition grew to the point where a personal clash became inevitable.

When Jesus announced to His supporters that He was going to Jerusalem for the Passover, they regarded it as going right into the enemy's trap. That's where the opposition was most keen.

3. *Instant Acclamation*

The prophet Zechariah, during the days of Darius the King of Persia 500 years before Christ, had prophesied, "Lo, your king comes to you; triumphant and victorious is he, humble and riding on an ass, on a colt the foal of an ass" (9:9b). To most, this prophecy had always been a problem. They had forgotten the ancient traditions. Biblical literature suggests that an unridden ass colt was the mount of the ancient rulers in Israel before the days of the horse. But ever since the days of King Solomon, the ass was regarded as a timid animal—a symbol of peace!

Israel was longing for a king. Those who had any messianic hope left had seen too many oppressors already. In Jesus' day, they had to put up daily with the disgusting presence of the Romans. They were weary of yoke after yoke.

Zechariah's prophecy would have spelled more hope if only he had predicted that the king would come on a horse—the new symbol of power and war! Then, perhaps, there might still be hope.

Jesus had told His disciples that He must suffer and die and that He would be raised from the dead. They had all been unable to understand this strange talk.

And so they arrived at Jerusalem on Palm Sunday for the historic Passover Feast. The crowded city was celebrating their deliverance at the Red Sea—it had been accomplished by the drowning of their Egyptian enemies.

Surely it must have stirred a new yearning for a fresh display of those "good old days." The mood was festive.

Jesus had "set his face to go to Jerusalem" (Luke 9:51b). He seemed to fear no opposition even though His disciples warned Him of the possible consequences.

But then word got around—*Jesus of Nazareth is coming to Jerusalem!* Some whispered that He might be the long-awaited Messiah, God's Anointed One. Others who had seen and heard of the miracles, dreamed that He might be the coming King who would reestablish political independence and Jerusalem would again be a great capital. Rumor spread wildly. Embers of hope became sparks of fire. Yearnings, long dormant, sprang to attention.

Masses turned to mobs. The roadside began to vibrate with an unexpected pulse.

Then Jesus came riding into sight—on a donkey!

The disciples didn't miss the connection with Zechariah's prophecy and neither did the mobs. The crowd's pitch rose to a high fever. Some frantically waved palm branches in salute to their hero. Others spread garments and leaves in His path. As the first-century equivalent of a ticker-tape parade wound up Jerusalem's "Broadway," there was a smell of history in the making! The whole multitude began to rejoice and praise God with a loud voice, "Hosanna! Blessed is he who comes in the name of the Lord, even the King of Israel!" (John 12:13b). "Blessed be the King who comes in the name of the Lord! Peace in heaven and glory in the highest!" (Luke 19:38).

Can you imagine the scene? Jesus had been dogged, tested, and criticized, especially the last two years of His public ministry. And now at the gates to the Holy City,

He was given instant acclamation. Even His most bitter enemies, the Pharisees, acknowledged His kingship for that day, saying to one another, "You see that you can do nothing; look, the world has gone after him" (John 12:19).

Jesus was instantly and overwhelmingly acclaimed King of kings and Lord of lords. It was the greatest day in Palestine since David had last driven out the Philistines. On that Palm Sunday, for one day, Jesus was King!

4. *Second Thoughts*

As a teenage boy, I took my first summer job away from home. Like other boys, I soon began to think seriously about my own set of "wheels." Every day after work, I visited the used-car lots. One day I spotted "it." I made a down payment and felt proud to own my very first car. I was to come back the next day to complete the arrangements for picking it up.

By the next morning I was thinking about the monthly payments, finance charges, insurance, license, and other expenses. I changed my mind. The dealer told me I'd lose the down payment. But I stood by my second thoughts! I realized that my first judgment had been hasty.

Have you ever caught yourself in a similar situation?

The Jerusalem crowds were ecstatic when Jesus rode into the city in seeming direct fulfilment of prophecy. It had all the appearances of a *sure thing;* it was too obvious to be coincidence. *This must* be God honoring His promise through His Holy Spirit. They were participating in the making of history. But their judgments were very hasty.

The acclaim must have seemed ironic to Jesus from the start. He knew that most people misunderstood His total mission and ministry. He knew that they adored Him because they expected Him to change and somehow to become exactly what *they* were waiting for.

First thing when Jesus drew near to Jerusalem He wept over the city and its misconceived thinking (Luke 19:41). He overturned the tables of the money changers and drove the traders from the temple (Luke 19:45). He cursed the unfruitful fig tree (Mark 11:14).

The mob began to settle down and to rethink the situation. *Their* King was going to drive out Romans—not their own religious leaders. *Their* King was going to *bless them* and *persecute their enemies*. Upon second thought, maybe this Jesus wasn't all that they supposed Him to be. Maybe He was an imposter! Surely, even if the Jewish leaders had shortcomings, the Romans were so much worse that Jesus should get after the "bad guys."

Their wreaths turned to wrath. Cheers become boos. Hosannas turned into hoots of ridicule. Laughter degenerated into mockery. Glad shouts slipped into bitter denunciation.

One day He was their King. The next day He became Public Enemy, No. 1. And so they began to plot and scheme. They tried hard to find a just cause for denunciation. Is there a greater wrath than that of hopes squashed hopelessly? In the guilt of man's fickleness there exists a tremendous passion for revenge.

Instant acclamation had been false acclamation. Jesus was not who nor what they had expected. And of course, *they* couldn't be wrong. It had to be Jesus who was wrong.

Yesterday they had thoughtlessly and impulsively

made Him King for one day. Today they just as thoughtlessly and impulsively condemned Him. Man is a fickle
creature. Jurisprudence says that any person is innocent
until proved guilty. Yet we so readily settle for gossip and
rumor. Their second thoughts were not based on serious
reflection of the consequences. They swung with the
mob yesterday and did so again today.

On Palm Sunday, the crowds acclaimed Jesus as the
one who could bring them new life. A day later, they saw
Him as the one who deserved death. A matter of life became a matter of death in just a few hours.

That Jerusalem crowd is a classic example of mob
psychology. People blow with the wind and play with life
and death.

Have you ever been caught in this trap?

5. *Jesus Is Our King for Every Day*

The Sunday following Palm Sunday is Easter. Once
again, churches will be filled to capacity. Christians will
again proclaim Jesus as King for the day.

But what of the days and weeks that follow?

One of the beautiful innovations for home cooking is
Teflon. It helps to give utensils a "no-stick" quality.

One of the serious maladies of the church is the
"Teflon-mind"—the mind that really sticks to nothing!
Truth is handled as a means to personal gain. Falsehood
gets equal billing with truth when personally expedient.
The "Teflon-mind" is always at the mercy of the latest
propaganda, gossip hysteria, or personal whim.

Paul Galdone in *Henny Penny* (Seabury Press, 1968)
retells the old Mother Goose story: Henny Penny is hit
on the head with an acorn. Her "Teflon-mind" concludes that "the sky is falling." She races around to

Cocky Locky, Ducky Lucky, Goosey Loosey, and Turkey Lurkey. They're all great names for "Teflon-minds." All follow the hysteria.

Then they meet Foxy Loxy who capitalizes on their fickleness. He will show them a shortcut to the king's palace. And they all follow without question.

The story concludes: "From that day to this, Turkey Lurkey, Goosey Loosey, Ducky Lucky, Cocky Locky, and Henny Penny have never been seen again. And the king has never been told the sky is falling. But Foxy Loxy and Mrs. Foxy Loxy and their seven little foxes still remember the fine feast they had that day."

Isn't that a good illustration of how the devil capitalizes on our fickleness? People readily say, "Lord, Lord," but fail to do the will of the Father in heaven. Those who follow any Henny Penny who comes along are destined in the end to be devoured by Foxy Loxy.

We as Christians wait for Jesus to come among us again. Are we like the Jews of the first century, still looking for a spectacular Messiah who will wipe out unemployment, inflation, recession, poverty, prejudice, political mistrust, the energy crises, and all our other assorted ills?

For you and me, Jesus is our King today and every day. But His kingdom is not made of Teflon, or of gold, or of bright lights, or of enthusiastic flag-waving crowds. Such people are notoriously fickle. One day they shout "Hosanna"—the next day it's "Crucify Him!" The kingdom of Jesus Christ is a kingdom of the heart—of our innermost being—the mind, the spirit, and the emotions.

Jesus Christ is King and Lord not by prestige and power, but by voluntary commitment of the self. He becomes our Master by our choice. He guides and directs every area of our living as we invite Him to.

Jesus Christ is Savior, but not Teflon-style. Nor does He makes us into perfect beings. He is our Savior because we need Him and ask Him to be. His salvation makes it possible for us to live because when we fail He is willing and able to forgive. You and I can live because He lives.

Jesus Christ can be our King today and every day.

The Towel and
the Basin

Extol the Love of Christ

Extol the love of Christ, ye saints,
And sing His wondrous worth,
Whose love, like God, eternal is
In heaven and on earth.
From God He brought His blessing rare;
To God He did ascend;
And constant in His heav'nly love
He loved unto the end.

Extol the love which sought to show
The Father's boundless grace;
The Son, from Father's bosom come,
Beheld the Father's face:
In servile garments clothed upon,
With humble service meet,
The Master loved as none could love
And washed His servants' feet.

Let poor, vain man example take
And from his pride repent;
For Christ far greater is than man,
Or servant that is sent.
Example, worthy, Christ has given,
And happy shall they be
Who wash each other's feet, and love
As deep and true as He.

—Samuel Frederick Coffman

John Mackay *said that the two greatest symbols of the church are the cross and the towel. The one means salvation; the other, service. One cannot have one without the other.*

4

THE TOWEL AND THE BASIN

By Howard J. Zehr

*If I then, your Lord and Teacher, have washed your feet,
you also ought to wash one another's feet. John 13:14.*

An unusual incident in the life of our Lord is recorded
in John 13. This account of Jesus washing His disciples'
feet reveals as much about Him as any other one passage
in the Scriptures. Yet many Bible students tend to pass
over this passage rather lightly.

Since it is recorded by the Apostle John it may be helpful to look at John's purpose for writing. That purpose is
well summarized later in the book: "Now Jesus did many
other signs in the presence of the disciples, which are not
written in this book; but these are written that you may
believe that Jesus is the Christ, the Son of God, and that
believing you may have life in his name" (20:30, 31).
John selected this incident in the life of our Lord de-

Howard J. Zehr, Elkhart, Indiana, pastored churches in Illinois and Indiana.
Much of his ministry was in executive responsibilities in the denomination. His
most recent assignment was as associate secretary of the Mennonite Board of
Congregational Ministries, Elkhart, Indiana, working in the areas of
leadership and evangelism. He died of cancer on July 13, 1977.

liberately to fulfill his intended purpose in writing.

This passage helps us to understand who Jesus is and what He is calling us to be. It reveals both the mission and method of our Lord. It tells us what He is about in this world. He came that we might have life through believing in Him. He came to reveal the character and will of the Father in heaven. The manner in which He came and the content of His teachings were drastically different from that which was anticipated. John says of Him, "He came to his own home, and his own people received him not" (1:11). Because He did not appear in the royal manner they had expected He was rejected by the masses. He rather came in humility and as a servant.

The real thrust of this passage is most frequently missed. Many scholars have conjectured about its meaning and significance for us in our life today. There seems to be a wide variety of opinions in this regard. A few groups have tended to interpret it quite literally and especially the words of Jesus where he concludes by saying, "If you know these things, blessed are you if you do them."

1. The Scene in the Upper Room

The occasion of this incident was our Lord's last night with His disciples as they were gathered together in the upper room. They were there to observe the Passover meal prior to Christ's death. John is the only writer who records the incident. It is interesting to observe that John is the only Gospel writer who doesn't record the institution of the Lord's Supper. John mentions that this happening took place during supper, but whether this refers to the Passover meal or to the instituted supper itself doesn't seem too significant. It is significant to note, however, that John mentions that they were gathered around the table for a meal together. During that meal Jesus arose, girded Himself with an apron towel, took the basin of water, and began to wash to the disciples' feet.

The washing of feet of guests was not a new experience. It was deeply engrained in ancient customs. Provision was always made for the washing of the feet of guests upon their arrival. A household servant was usually charged with the responsibility of washing the feet of the guests upon their arrival or at least was responsible to have a basin of water and a towel available.

Seemingly no provision had been made on this occasion, even though we are told that Jesus had sent two of His disciples ahead to prepare for the Passover meal. We recall from the other Gospel writers that there had been contention among the disciples as to who should be the greatest. It could well be that no one among them was willing to assume this servant role on this occasion. But Jesus arose from the table, girded Himself with the apron towel, took the basin of water, and began to wash the disciples' feet.

2. The Impact of This Dramatic Act

One can hardly imagine the impact this must have had upon the disciples. It was only a short time prior to this that they were disputing among themselves as to who should be the greatest in the kingdom, and the mother of James and John had requested that her two sons might be seated one on the right hand and one on the left of Jesus in His eternal kingdom. Since they had not caught the significance of Jesus' coming and the heart of His message, He here dramatizes His teaching for them.

Again and again he had emphasized that the way to true
greatness is the way of service. The way to real life is
through a willingness to die. We receive by giving.

3. Jesus' Illustrative Act

As Jesus washed the feet of the disciples and wiped
them with the towel He was illustrating all that He had
taught and the central purpose of His coming. The laying aside of His outer garment was symbolic of the way
He had laid aside the glory which was His with the
Father in order to become the Servant of men. As Paul
put it in Philippians 2 He emptied Himself, took upon
Him the form of a servant, and was obedient to death,
even the death of the cross. Then God highly exalted
Him and gave Him a name which is above every name
that at the name of Jesus every knee should bow.

John began to describe this incident by emphasizing
that "Jesus knew that his hour had come to depart out of
this world to the Father, having loved his own who were
in the world, he loved them to the end. And during supper, when the devil had already put it into the heart of
Judas Iscariot, Simon's son, to betray him, Jesus, knowing that the Father had given all things into his hands,
and that he had come from God and was going to God,
rose from supper, laid aside his garments, and girded
himself with a towel. Then he poured water into a basin,
and began to wash the disciples' feet, and to wipe them
with the towel with which he was girded."

It is clear that Jesus did all this in full consciousness of
His mission in the world. He performed this dramatic act
fully conscious of who He was and what He had come to
accomplish in the world. He had come to be the Savior
and the Servant of all mankind. He humbled Himself to

identify fully with us in our predicament, to give us life eternal, and to show us the true way.

4. *The Encounter with Simon Peter*

This must have indeed been a bewildering experience for the disciples. However, seemingly none of them objected until Jesus came to wash the feet of Peter. Outspoken as he was, Peter likely verbalized the sentiments of the group who lacked the courage to express their true feelings. Peter was always very open and honest about himself. Therefore, as Jesus came to wash his feet, Peter said, "You shall never wash my feet."

But Jesus answered, "If I do not wash you, you have no part in me."

These words impressed Peter deeply so he said, "Lord, not my feet only but also my hands and my head!"

Then Jesus replied to him, "He who has bathed does not need to wash, except for his feet, but he is clean all over; and you are clean, but not all of you." Then John comments, "For he knew who was to betray him; that was why he said, 'You are not all clean.' "

5. *What Meaning for Us?*

Jesus' reply to Peter gives us a real clue to what Jesus was dramatically portraying. It was the practice in the ancient orient for guests to bathe before gathering at the home of the host. But it was still necessary for them to have their feet washed upon arrival to remove the dirt which had gathered from walking the dusty roads of Palestine. It wasn't necessary to have a complete bath upon arrival, for they had already bathed before coming. But to be clean they needed this dust from their dirty feet removed.

Here is indeed a symbol of Christ's work for us.
Through faith in Him we are cleansed from all of our sin.
However, we live in a sinful world. Our Lord has com-
missioned us to go into this world to live and to share the
good news. As we do this we risk becoming contaminated
with this world and its evils. But Jesus' provision is for
this also.

John said in his epistle, "But if we walk in the light, as
he is in the light, we have fellowship with one another,
and the blood of Jesus his Son cleanses us from all sin" (1
John 1:7). Christ's work for us continues to cleanse and to
renew us in our life day by day.

6. Our Responsibility to Each Other

After Jesus had washed their feet, taken His garments
again, and resumed His place at the table, He asked,
"Do you know what I have done to you? You call me
Teacher and Lord; and you are right, for so I am. If I
then, your Lord and Teacher, have washed your feet, you
also ought to wash one another's feet. For I have given
you an example, that you also should do as I have done to
you. Truly, truly, I say to you, a servant is not greater
than his master; nor is he who is sent greater than he who
sent him. If you know these things, blessed are you if you
do them."

Notice that Jesus said, "If I then, your Lord and
Teacher have washed your feet, you also ought to wash
one another's feet." This word "ought" comes from the
word in the original text which means to be placed under
obligation to be servants one to another. Jesus said, "If I
your Lord and Master have washed your feet, you are
under obligation to wash one another's feet. How do we
do that in today's world?

7. Servants Not Masters; Servanthood Not Just Service

The call of Jesus is a call to commitment, a commitment to servanthood. It is not simply *doing* service but it is *being* a servant. This is not a one-time act but it is a way of life. Jesus came down from heaven, emptied Himself of His glory with the Father to redeem us from our sins. He calls us to give up ourselves, to follow Him in serving one another.

The besetting sins of this world so easily overtake us. To be faithful to the mission of Christ calls for risks. If we are going to be faithful we cannot live in isolation from the world and its sins. We may not always keep ourselves free from its contamination. The act of Jesus on the cross not only saves us from our sins as a one-time act but provides for us a continuing cleansing experience. As we noted earlier from John's epistle, "If we walk in the light, as he is in the light, we have fellowship with one another, and the blood of Jesus his Son cleanses us from all sin" (1 John 1:7). The word *cleanses* is in the so-called imperfect tense in the original Greek which has the meaning of continuous action. Thus the work of Jesus keeps cleansing us from our sins.

8. Some Implications for Us

Jesus told the disciples that if He did this for them, they were under obligation to relate to each other in the same way. What implications might this have for us in our Christian lives and experiences?

It impresses me that Jesus is laying upon us the responsibility for one another. We have an obligation to help each other as brothers and sisters in our pilgrim walk and as we try to be faithful disciples of our Lord. When we fail, we need each other's help. We need the stimulation, the encouragement, the empathy, and the support of our brothers and sisters when we fail.

Jesus places us under obligation to care, to identify with one another in our struggles, and to help each other even when we fall. We have a responsibility to help each other experience the redeeming grace of our Lord Jesus Christ.

The Lord calls us to be servants to one another. Let us therefore not only serve, but also commit ourselves to a life of servanthood.

The Crucifixion and the
Political Powers

I simply argue that the cross be raised again at the center of the marketplace as well as on the steeple of the church. I am recovering the claim that Jesus was not crucified in a cathedral between two candles, but on a cross between two thieves; on the town garbage heap, at a crossroads so cosmopolitan that they had to write his title in Hebrew and in Latin and in Greek (or shall we say in English, in Bantu, and in Afrikaans?); at the kind of place where cynics talk smut, and thieves curse, and soldiers gamble. Because that is where He died. And that is what He died about. And that is where churchmen should be and what churchmen should be about.

—George F. Macleod in
Only One Way Left

5

THE CRUCIFIXION AND THE POLITICAL POWERS

By Howard H. Charles

Pilate entered the praetorium again and called Jesus, and said to him, "Are you the King of the Jews?" John 18:33.

Most people do not think of the cross in political terms. For many it belongs to an almost unworldly realm. Although it has its earthly side, the proper approach to its understanding is thought to be from above rather than from beneath. It calls for a theological explanation rather than historical causation. It is an integral part of the language of faith and devotion. To speak of it as a political event seems inappropriately secular.

To be sure, we have not said everything about the cross that needs to be said when we speak of it as the product of forces within history. It is the spiritual dimension that makes the cross of Golgotha unique among all the crosses planted in Palestine in the first century. But

Howard H. Charles, Goshen, Indiana, has served as pastor and on numerous denominational committees and boards. He has had teaching ministries in Japan and Ghana and since 1947 has taught at Goshen College and Goshen Biblical Seminary. Presently he is professor of New Testament at Associated Mennonite Biblical Seminaries, Elkhart, Indiana.

the cross also has horizontal roots. Unless these are given due attention, the full historical character of the cross is lost to view. And with that eclipse the true meaning of the incarnation is threatened.

1. Climax of a Career

The death of Jesus must not be separated from His total life. It was not an isolated event but the climax of a career. It was the death of One who lived and ministered in Roman controlled Palestine. The political character of Jesus' death is broadly evident from two facts.

First, He was put to death by crucifixion. This was a Roman and not a Jewish method of execution. It is clear both from Christian and Roman sources that Jesus was crucified by the Roman state.

Second, the charge that was posted over His cross was written by the Roman governor, Pilate. According to Mark 15:26 the text read, "The King of the Jews." This was a political accusation. Rome had a king and there was no room for another. Rightly or wrongly, Jesus was put to death as a political subversive.

For details with regard to this charge, we must look to the gospel records of the trial before Pilate. These accounts vary in fullness and in detail. But all four Gospels indicate that political issues were at stake. These are spelled out most clearly in Luke 23:2. Jesus' countrymen accused Him of "perverting our nation, and forbidding us to give tribute to Caesar, and saying that he himself is Christ a king." In the other Gospels the first two items are not mentioned. But all four accounts represent Pilate as questioning Jesus on the matter of kingship (Matthew 27:11; Mark 15:2; Luke 23:3; John 18:33-37).

If the matter of kingship appears in the trial of Jesus

before Pilate, it is also clear that the Gospels point to some hesitation on Pilate's part in passing the death sentence on Jesus. This is most strongly present in Luke and John. In each of these there is a threefold witness to the innocence of Jesus (Luke 23:4, 14, 22; John 18:38; 19:4, 6). Indeed, in John's Gospel, Pilate is represented as having his hand forced by the Jewish threat to accuse him of being a traitor to Caesar if he did not execute Jesus. Jesus was officially tried, condemned, and executed by Rome's representative in Palestine on the charge of political subversion to the state.

The story becomes somewhat complicated when one moves behind the Roman court scene to the preliminary proceedings against Jesus by the Jewish authorities. All four Gospels report such activity but again with varying fullness and detail. But all bear witness to two facts: (1) the Jewish authorities had a hand in Jesus' arrest and (2) they conducted some sort of examination of Jesus. In John it has the appearance of an investigation while in the Synoptics it resembles a trial. In Mark (14:64) and in Matthew (26:66) Jesus was formally sentenced to death by the Jewish authorities on the charge of blasphemy. This additional detail is absent from Luke and John.

2. A Grand Jury Inquiry

In attempting to sort out what actually happened, the following reconstruction is offered for consideration. The action of the Jewish authorities between the time of the arrest and transferring Jesus over to Pilate can perhaps be described most accurately as a kind of grand jury proceeding. It was to gather data with a view to formulating a case against Jesus.

Although in Mark and in Matthew a trial scene leads

to a formal sentence, it is clear that the Jewish authorities did not dispose of Jesus themselves because they lacked the power of capital punishment. This fact is asserted in John 18:31. Historians who have studied Roman provincial law have also arrived at this conclusion. Rome reserved the right of passing capital sentence for the chief administrative officer of the province. In the case of Judea this was the procurator. The only exception to this general policy was in the case of free cities within the empire. There the death sentence and its execution was in local hands. But Jerusalem was not a free city and thus did not have this right.

3. A Twofold Problem

The Jewish authorities faced a twofold problem. On the one hand, to get the Roman governor's approval to execute Jesus, a charge valid from Rome's standpoint would need to be brought against Him. A religious charge would not be sufficient. But political treason, if established, would bring the desired action. On the other hand, the Jewish authorities had to discredit Jesus in the eyes of the people to avoid a popular reaction over His arrest. Jesus was not a nobody. He had a following. His reputation needed to be destroyed. This could be accomplished effectively if the religious charge of blasphemy were brought against Him. This was done in the Jewish proceedings prior to the Roman trial. See Mark 14:55-64 and parallels.

It is clear then that the complex religious-political situation sheds light on two features in the proceedings against Jesus: (1) it explains why the Sanhedrin having pronounced sentence on Jesus subsequently became the prosecutor in Pilate's court seeking to win a verdict against Him and (2) it helps us to understand the shift from the religious to the political charge as the trial moves from a Jewish to a Roman setting.

4. *The Charge Is Unclear*

The grounds for a religious charge of blasphemy are not entirely clear. A claim to messiahship would not in itself have been regarded as blasphemous. There must have been another basis. According to Mark (14:61) and Matthew (26:63), the high priest queried Jesus not only in regard to messiahship but also whether He was the Son of the Blessed (or God). In both of these passages the two titles (Messiah and Son of God) are used together suggesting a synonymous meaning. However, in Luke the high priest put two distinct questions to Jesus. They are separated from each other by intervening conversation (22:67-71). Apparently, the two titles are intended to carry different meanings. It was not messiahship so much as something more that was found objectionable by the Jewish leaders.

Elsewhere in the Gospels the charge of blasphemy is associated with certain claims that Jesus made that were regarded as inappropriate to man. Attention may be called to two of these. The one was the claim to forgive sins (Mark 2:5-7). The other was the right to call God His own special Father (John 5:16-18). It is possible that it was the latter concern that was echoed in the question, "Are you the Son of God?" (Luke 22:70).

5. *A Charge of Subversion?*

What shall we say about the political charge of subversion against the Roman state? Rome had a sensitive ear to charges of this sort, especially in such a potential trouble spot as Palestine. The relationship between the Jewish community and Rome from the time that Judea passed under direct Roman rule in AD 6 until the great war in AD 66-70 was one of more or less tension. Rome's general policy was one of toleration within limits. But some of the governors in Judea were less able to understand the Jewish spirit and were less flexible in dealing with the situation than others.

From the Jewish side, various stances were taken toward the Roman occupation. Broadly speaking, three may be identified.

a. There were those Jews who, although they preferred independence, were ready to collaborate with Rome in a more or less active way. Here mention may be made of the high priestly families and the lay aristocracy who held responsible posts under the Romans in the administration of affairs in Judea. There were also the Jewish publicans some of whom collected taxes from their countrymen for Herod Antipas of Galilee and others for the procurator in Judea. Reference may also be made to the Herodians (Mark 3:6; 12:13). They appear to have been active supporters of the Herodian rulers who were, of course, puppets of Rome.

b. At the other end of the spectrum were those who were dedicated to active resistance against Rome. They were ready to use violent methods to achieve Jewish independence. They are usually designated as the Zealots. This movement became increasingly influential in first-century Judaism and finally swept the nation into the great revolt of AD 66-70.

c. Between these two extremes were Jews who neither cooperated to the extent of the publicans or the Sadducean aristocracy nor were ready to adopt a strategy of violent resistance. Most of the Jews, including the Pharisees and the Qumranites, belonged to this category.

Vigorous attempts have been made to associate Jesus with the Zealot stance. His crucifixion is then viewed as Rome's response to revolutionary tactics. But the evidence at hand does not support such a position. It points rather to a profoundly independent role which was alike critical of aspects of Sadduceeism, Pharisaism, and Zealotism. The leadership of Judaism could not tolerate His challenge and sought for ways to remove Him from the community. The double charge of religious and political subversion proved to be an effective method.

The Judgment of the People

Consider how helpful the opposition of the world may prove to be.

First it helps me realize more clearly that I belong to Christ. I am of the Master's family. If He is Lord, should I not expect the same treatment as He endured? So I'm not spared the pain of the cross. That's true. But neither am I denied the blessing of the cross, which assures me I am Christ's.

Second, suffering for Christ reveals my separateness from the world more clearly to others and to myself. When I can delight in the world's fare and worldly persons delight in me there can be little sense of real spiritual life. True witnesses of each generation know something of what it means that "all who will live godly in Christ Jesus must suffer persecution."

Persecution whether by fire or sword or slander or scorn, whether by publicity and contempt or quiet social ostracism, is still present to one who lives the Christ-life. If I do not experience, at least to some extent, the same response my Master met, I may well begin to ask myself whether my discipleship is real.

It is good to recall that Jesus said the reason the world hated Him was because He testified of it that its deeds were evil. What is wrong if the world feels I keep my proper place?

—John M. Drescher

6
THE JUDGMENT OF THE PEOPLE
By Katie Funk Wiebe

They cried out again. "Not this man, but Barabbas!" John 18:40.

The task: to sell twenty thousand boxes of chocolates at $2 each. And only four hundred high school boys to do it.

In *The Chocolate War* by Robert Cormier (Pantheon, 1974), the acting schoolmaster of the boys' school has doubled last year's quota of chocolates and the price. If the campaign succeeds and the school debt is liquidated through it, he sees a promotion ahead. So he pressures the boys to sell.

But one skinny little freshman, Jerry Renault, has looked too long at the poster in his locker which reads: "Do I dare disturb the universe?" He accepts at face value the teacher's words that the sale is voluntary. He refuses to sell chocolates and become the older man's pawn.

Katie Funk Wiebe, Hillsboro, Kansas, a well-known writer, is assistant professor of English and journalism at Tabor College in Hillsboro.

As the plot unfolds, the issue is no longer selling chocolates, but whether a power-hungry administrator can force the young boy to bend to him. The name of the game becomes power.

Jerry is harassed by obscene phone calls, subjected to public ridicule, and taunted in private by being called a fairy. His class assignments are stolen. Finally, his influence with other students is subdued by outright violence in a forced but mismatched boxing fight.

As he is carried to the ambulance, he tells his friend through broken lips to "do whatever they wanted you to do. . . . Don't disturb the universe whatever you do." The cost is too great. When someone wants power, give it to them. Shut up. Step aside. Whatever the majority decides is what you must do. Position means power. Numbers means power. A minority is invisible and defenseless against evil.

The story is tragic, for the young protagonist seems to have no recourse but to give in to evil.

1. Disturbing the Universe.

About two thousand years ago, another Person disturbed the universe. The name of the game at that time was also power. The Christ-man upset the equilibrium of the Sanhedrin, a group of men who were both the religious and civic authorities over the Jews. This council of elders was comprised of the wisest and most experienced men of the nation. In their group were priests, scribes, students of the law, wealthy and educated landowners, and businessmen. The Sanhedrin symbolized authority and power. They controlled the values of the common people because they were protectors of Jewish law and tradition.

Why was the hatred of the Jewish leaders toward Jesus so intense that they moved as one jet-propelled body toward their goal—to get rid of Him? Surely at previous times new teachers had sprung forth in Judea and attracted a following, thereby annoying the Sanhedrin. Why were they allowed live? We could also ask why the acting headmaster in the war of the chocolates found it impossible to overlook the puny freshman and his fifty unsold boxes of chocolates.

R. C. H. Lenski in *Interpretations of St. John's Gospel* (Lutheran Book Concern, 1942) suggests an answer: "Not for one moment did any of these superior men put confidence in Jesus. So old is the argument, which still is current, that in religious matters men of power, authority, and learning cannot err, and that all humbler people ought to be guided by them without question. It was the argument which the lone monk of Wittenberg had to face. Could he alone be right when the people, the emperor, and all the prelates and princes held the contrary view? Could he alone be right, and they all be wrong?"

Christ did not demand the allegiance of the Sanhedrin, but He did offer them salvation if they acknowledged Him as the Son of God. The thought was preposterous to them. Even blasphemous. They were holy men. They had truth, for they had the law. They didn't need Christ.

Jesus' teachings and acts made clear that the upholders of tradition must change their attitudes about the law, about people, about themselves, and particularly about Jesus as the Messiah. Jesus told them, "I am the way, the truth, and the life." He healed the sick. He forgave sins and freed people from religious bondage.

By His words and works Christ demonstrated an authority the Sanhedrin did not have—the power over
death, and therefore over life. After He restored Lazarus
to life, they became particularly fearful. How could they
keep their clout with such a man in their midst? He
represented a direct threat to their honor, popularity,
and influence as religious leaders. And power is usually
something those who have are not about to give up
voluntarily.

Persons do not normally yield authority and advantage, whether it has come to them naturally because
of race, sex, or social position, or was acquired through
education, election, business, or political acumen. And
those who have power have a natural tendency to take on
more. Even Pilate later knew that it was out of envy that
they had delivered Christ to him (Matthew 27:18).

So the Jewish leaders set themselves against Christ,
doubtless with the firm belief that in upholding tradition
and opposing His radical notions, they were virtuous
while He was committing the most heinous of crimes.
The evening before Christ was crucified, the members of
the Sanhedrin and the populace gathered before the
Roman ruler, Pilate, to make the final decision on what
should be done with Jesus, this man who made wild
claims about being Son of God and having the formula
for eternal life.

The Pharisees were sure they had life eternal without
Jesus (John 5:39). They didn't need this impostor. When
Pilate offered them a choice between Barabbas, an acknowledged insurrectionist, and Jesus, with one voice
they demanded that Barabbas be freed and Christ
crucified. And so Pilate delivered Jesus to them to be
crucified according to Roman law.

Yet even as the defeat of Jerry Renault was the result of a long process of harassment, so the death of Christ was the culmination of a long process of hate and violence stretching over three years. According to Jacques Ellul in *Violence* (Seabury Press, 1969), violence is always a process, which once begun cannot be stopped. Violence only begets more violence, unless mercy and forgiveness intervene.

2. *They Are Not Alone*

Though readers of the life of Christ do not usually identify with the Pharisees and Sadducees in their struggle with Jesus, for they are the acknowledged villains in this story—the bad guys—yet all humankind have inherited their methods and their goals and use them faithfully to this day.

Christ's ideas were too potent to be allowed to move freely in the territory of the Jewish leaders. They had the sting of truth. His mouth must be stopped and their own brand of truth established once again in the minds of the common people. As the Jews watched, He did miracles. They tried discrediting the miracles and criticizing Him for healing on the Sabbath. They argued with Him, but He bettered them in debate. The need to shut Him up permanently was clear or they would be eliminated. But how to do it?

They did it the same way we get rid of people today whose ideas disturb our universe, whether it is a tangle between neighbors over too many dandelions in a lawn, or between Christians in the church over the kind of music to play. Anyone who arouses our conscience to say, to be, to act more clearly for the gospel when we feel quite comfortable in the way we are living for God forces us to take some action to oust that person from his or her place of influence.

The first stage in silencing the disturbers of our inner peace is usually with words spoken to the person directly or behind his or her back. Blacks have been called "nigger" and "boy" to keep them in their place. In the ecclesiastical realm, terms like "fundie," "Bible-thumper," "liberal," "social gospeler," "sexist," or even "women's libber," are effective ways of disposing in our own minds of persons we don't like or want nothing to do with. By labeling them, we push them into a box we have created for them and think we have freed ourselves of them and their views.

Gossip, labeling, or belittling someone has always been an effective weapon in a psychological battle for power. The Pharisees could not disregard Jesus, for the people flocked to Him. Yet they found it difficult to speak to Him directly or to call Him by His right name, so they referred to Him as "this fellow." Lenski states this was a derogatory term used to keep Him in His place. The strong negative connotations of the phrase are lost by translating it as "this man." He is similarly referred to by the Jews in John 7:15, 35; and 11:47.

Ridicule was a common stance of the Jewish leaders during the first years of Jesus' ministry. At one point when many people believed on Him, the common people said, "When the Christ appears, will he do more signs than this man has done?" (John 7:31). The Pharisees overheard the people murmuring their belief.

When the officers whom the Sanhedrin had sent to apprehend Christ came back empty-handed, overawed by the power in Christ's words, the Pharisees scornfully derided them with "Are you led astray, you also?" And

they cursed the multitude, which knew not the law, for
believing Him. When Christ told them they would look
for Him and not find Him and that where He went, they
could not come, they replied mockingly. They pretended
to be mystified by His words. Where would He go, they
asked, that they would not be able to find Him (John
7:33, 34)? What a ridiculous statement for Him to make!

But even this condescending attitude toward Jesus did
not prevent Him from continuing His ministry, sometimes deliberately on the Sabbath to confront the Jewish
leaders. The people were attracted to the One who fed
them from a boy's lunch, turned water into wine, healed
their sick, and freed their souls from the prison of sin and
guilt.

Something more drastic had to be done. "If we let him
go on thus," said the leaders, "everyone will believe in
him, and the Romans will come and destroy both our
holy place and our nation" (John 11:48). What an admission of the real issue—not truth, but power.

Jacques Ellul writes that violence is all of one kind
whether it is physical or psychological. Christ told His
followers that to hate was the same as to kill (Matthew
5:21, 22). The hatred of the Jewish leaders shifted from
the psychological realm to its natural conclusion—
physical violence.

The incident which gave the Jews the opportunity to
flex their religious muscles and to show the people they
still had much power was the healing of the man who was
born blind. The young man's parents feared the religious
authorities so much, they would answer no questions put
to them about him, but told the rulers to ask their son.
Outraged by the healed man's simplistic answers ("Once
I was blind, but now I can see"), they expelled him from

the synagogue, making good the threat they had uttered earlier to anyone who confessed that Jesus was the Christ.

Lenski states that such expulsion had serious civil and social ramifications. The excommunicated one was treated as an apostate or accursed and shut off from religious communion with the Jews as well as from the hopes, blessings, and promises of Israel. He became as a pagan, a frightening state for the orthodox Jew, so people obeyed the Sanhedrin out of fear. In numerous passages, the fear of the Jews on the part of the common people is mentioned (John 7:33; 9:22, 19:38; 20:19). Even after the resurrection this fear was still very real. The disciples gathered in an upper room behind closed doors for fear of the Jews (John 21:19).

3. Background Is Absent

The battle for truth on the part of Christ and power on the part of the Jews took another twist. They employed a technique used frequently when some authority in a professional role does not wish to admit that the person in blue jeans and T-shirt may be right and he may be wrong. The Sanhedrin charged Jesus with incompetency and lack of proper qualifications to be a great religious teacher. "How is it that this man has learning, when he has never studied?" (John 7:15).

To be a spokesman for truth, surely one must have at least a doctor of philosophy degree or two, or be a pastor or a member of an important committee or board! To come from one of the leading church families and have a little money helps also.

The Sanhedrin tried to shift the question from "How true is his teaching?" to "What schools did he attend?"

Which seminary did he graduate from? Is it liberal or conservative? If of none, how dare he speak? If he has no professional qualifications as a theologian, he should shut up, for God speaks only through persons who have the necessary qualifications, not through an unlearned person. They attempted to maintain their position by knocking down and discrediting the One who challenged their authority.

On the final evening when the struggle between the Sanhedrin and Christ climaxed, the characters in the drama were Jesus, Pilate, the high priest and elders, Barabbas, and the people. Once before the Pharisees had attempted to get rid of Jesus by stoning him (John 8:59), but He had slipped from them. Now they were sure they had Him secure.

Jesus' threats to their position as religious authority over the people would soon be over. Marshall McLuhan writes that "when one has been hurt by a new technology, when the private person or corporate body finds its entire identity endangered by physical or psychic change, it lashes back in a fury of self-defense (quoted in *The Dust of Death* by Os Guinness, Inter-varsity, 1973). And now for the last time the Jews struck back. Viciously. Thoroughly, they thought. Jesus would not escape them again.

But they had not counted on Pilate's inability to make a decision. Pilate faced a dilemma. One Man before him was innocent of any guilt, and he knew it. The other man condemned to die was guilty, and he also knew that. But unable to stand by his own convictions, he abandoned his task as judge and gave the people the opportunity to decide the case.

Clearly Pilate expected the people to have higher standards of justice than he had himself, so he set before them a proposition involving two obvious unequals. He was following a Passover custom in offering the Jews the choice of setting one prisoner free. He was sure they would want the man who was a criminal to be crucified. He appealed to the majority of the people milling about before him to decide what should have been his decision.

If power corrupts, so does powerlessness. At this crucial moment the Man the Jews had bribed Judas to betray with 30 pieces of silver, the Man whose death seemed so certain, looked as if He might again be freed to influence the people. What to do?

Quickly the Sanhedrin moved among the people and stirred them up with a few stories and persuaded them to ask that Barabbas be freed. The people agreed. They answered Pilate's questions regarding whom he should free with a roar of voices which became a chant, "Crucify, crucify him." The majority had spoken. The people had judged. And Pilate accepted their verdict. And to the present moment many kinds of injustices are still allowed in the name of majority rule.

4. Why Were the People Fickle?

Only a few days earlier on Palm Sunday these same people had been waving palm leaves and shouting "Hosanna" as they followed their newly acknowledged King through the streets. They gave Him a royal welcome. They had been excited by His promises of becoming their Messiah, which they interpreted to mean an earthly ruler. Now as they stood before Pilate, their words mocked Him. Why?

Fear may have been one reason—fear of the Jewish leaders and what they might do to those who disobeyed them. Yet they may have recognized their own mistake. Jesus was no king. Kings were not tried like common criminals. Kings had power and glory and majesty and led their people to victory, not to the cross.

But the reason for their fickleness may also have been that the climate of opinion for or against a person is sometimes so infectious that those who are involved in a conflict take the attitudes of the main body for granted. Eric Hoffer, the longshoreman philosopher, writes in *The True Believer* that the follower of mass movements does not examine issues. He leaves some ecclesiastic (priest, minister) the major task to define spiritual responsibility for him.

When Pilate asked his question, the populace allowed the Sanhedrin to tell them what was truth. Though the elders had cursed the people at one time for blindly following Christ, now the common people allowed themselves to be used by these elders to bring about the desired decision. The elders were in charge, therefore they knew best.

The people accepted the word of their religious leaders in somewhat the same way as Hitler's Germany accepted their Fuehrer's words that Germany must become a pure race. The Pharisees said they were holy men. The law and tradition had been their specialties for centuries. Therefore they must be right. This Man in purple robe and crown of thorns was such a newcomer.

So the majority determined what should be done, and the record does not show that anyone contradicted that common voice. To stand with Jesus in Pilate's hall meant to stand with a minority of one. To stand with the Sanhedrin meant to side with a large, comfortable majority in which one's personal identity would never be revealed.

Consequently, the people spoke for themselves, for their children, for religious authority, and for civic government, "We want Christ crucified."

Only one thing was left—the actual crucifixion—and that the Jews had to allow the Roman soldiers to do while they watched. Os Guinness writes in *The Dust of Death* (Inter-Varsity, 1973) that violence brings its own catharsis. In their decision to crucify Christ, the people were asserting they had discovered their own way of finding freedom and meaning in life. With the words, "Crucify him," they were saying, "We are free of this man and his claims upon us." Guinness writes that violence makes a person fearless and restores new hope, new life, new ideals, and new self-respect.

By killing the Christ-man, the Pharisees could proclaim He was not their Messiah. Now they were sure of this fact. If He was who He claimed to be, He would have asserted Himself by now. By morning the whole trauma would be over. They could return to the celebration of the Passover—sure of their authority over the people, and with the further knowledge that the evening's activities had not even defiled them ceremonially. They were still clean.

Christ went to the cross. But it was not a chocolate cross, such as we give to children at Easter, nor was the war a chocolate war. Jerry Renault, the high school boy, dared to defy the school administrator but found he lacked strength to overcome. Christ chose death at the hands of His enemies and became the victor.

When tried by Pilate, he spoke plainly: "My kingship is not of this world" (John 18:36). He accepted the death of the cross but was vindicated by the resurrection, His final proof to the Sanhedrin that He was the way, the truth, and the life. By His resurrection He broke forever the power of men to enslave others through the use of the law and tradition. In exchange He offered those who would be free a cross. "If anyone wishes to be a follower of mine, he must leave self behind; he must take up his cross and come with me" (Matthew 16:24, NEB).

For every person a cross. Not Christ's cross, but his own. Each must choose to bear it. It is never thrust upon anyone. It is only for the one who wishes to be a follower of Christ's. A majority decision may have sent Christ to His cross, but salvation and discipleship are always personal decisions.

The Word of the Cross

Golgotha

I heard two soldiers talking as they
came down the hill—

The somber hill of Calvary—bleak,
and black and still;

And one said: "The night is dark;
these thieves take long to die!"

And one said: "I am sore afraid; and
yet I know not why!"

I heard two women weeping as down
the hill they came,

And one was like a broken rose, and
one was like a flame.

And one said, "Men shall rue this
deed their hands have done!"

And one cried only, through her
tears: "My Son, my Son, my Son!"

—Theodosia Garrison

7

THE WORD OF THE CROSS

By Marlin E. Miller

For the word of the cross is folly to those who are perishing,
but to us who are being saved it is the power of God. 1 Corin-
thians 1:18.

The Apostle Paul sometimes summarized the gospel as
the "word of the cross." Far from narrowing the New
Testament message down to a handy cliché, this short
phrase binds together the life of Jesus and the early
church, the work of Christ and Christian conduct. The
"word of the cross" is rooted in a particular historic
event, signifies the forgiveness of sins through Jesus
Christ, points to the faithfulness and sacrifice of Jesus
Christ on our behalf, and symbolizes the Christian
lifestyle in the world.

Many religions zealously tally the number of miracles
wrought by their founders and followers; only the New
Testament proclaims the cross of Christ as the decisive

Marlin E. Miller, Elkhart, Indiana, served in peace work, congregational
leadership, and as resource person in Europe and West Africa from 1968-1974.
Since 1974 he has been associate professor of theology and president of Goshen
Biblical Seminary, Elkhart, Indiana.

act of God. Many religions recount stories of divine beings taking on human form; only the Christian faith focuses on God Incarnate suffering the ignominious death on the cross.

Several religions hope for life after death; only the Christian hope lives from the resurrection of the Crucified One. Little wonder that the apostle reminds his readers that the "word of the cross" appears as foolishness and weakness in the eyes of the world.

1. Human Power and Wisdom

In the early chapters of 1 Corinthians, Paul emphasized one facet of this unique word of the cross. The Corinthian Christians had apparently relegated the cross to the margin of faith and life. In their perhaps even well-intentioned enthusiasm for the gospel, they had translated the word of the cross into categories compatible with the wisdom and power coveted by the society around them. They may even have replaced the message of the cross with Corinthian versions of human power and wisdom.

The consequences were devastating. Instead of welding Christians of diverse ethnic and religious origins into a new community in Christ, conformity to Corinthian wisdom and power began to fragment the young congregation. Instead of shaping a Christian lifestyle which could be a light in a religiously and morally decadent society, the conformity to Corinthian wisdom and power added a halo to the immorality and justified it in the name of Christian liberty.

In this context, the apostle vigorously called the Corinthian Christians back to the centrality of the cross. Conformity to the cross and nonconformity to the surrounding society would lead to church unity and faithful Christian conduct; nonconformity to the cross and conformity to the surrounding society would deepen the congregational divisions and undermine Christian obedience.

Let us look more closely at why and how the Christians at Corinth departed from the "word of the cross" because of conformity to the surrounding culture and society.

2. *Why Did Early Christians Change Their Thinking?*

The Corinthian Christians were doubtless impressed by the many philosophical "schools" and groups in their city. Each had its wise teacher who vied with others in thinking the deepest thoughts and attracting the most brilliant students. These philosophers taught the latest fads as well as the most venerated traditions. They sought to give a wise and profound account of human experience, about the world of nature and society.

Many of the Corinthian Christians apparently transferred the customs of Christian "schools" and groups to the church. They saw Paul, Peter, and Apollos as their wise men, each bringing new insights and teaching. The Corinthian church, who had little educational or social standing, could now boast about "their philosopher." They could also be "somebody." Like other groups in Corinth they began to argue the merits of "their" teachers and the demerits of the others. One group boasted of Paul, but *not* Peter as their wise man. Another claimed Peter, but *not* Paul as theirs. One group even claimed Christ, but *not* either Paul or Peter or Apollos as theirs.

The congregation thus became a reflection of the Corinthian pagan society—divided into groups which disputed conflicting claims of wisdom and loyalty to their "wise man." Conformity to the wisdom of the world around them threatened to divide the congregation permanently.

This conformity to the society and the nonconformity to the cross expressed itself not only in the congregational relations, but almost certainly in the content of the message as well. As an illustration of how Christians of Greek origins would have valued wisdom and how sophisticated non-Christians would have therefore criticized the "word of the cross," we may refer to Celsus' attack on Christianity.

Celsus, even though writing a generation after the Apostle Paul, spoke out of the same mentality which would have been present in first-century Corinth. He vigorously tried to demonstrate the utter senselessness of the cross. Celsus recognized that the Christians proclaimed "the Son of God to be the Word." But for the Greek philosopher, *Word* represented beauty, goodness, and the profound rationality of reality.

The Word preached by the Christians by contrast grated Celsus' sensibilities and challenged reasonable standards of truth. He disdained those "who do not bring forth a true and holy Word, but a man who was arrested most disgracefully and crucified." Had Jesus been genuinely divine—Celsus argued—He should have displayed His divine power and greatness by "suddenly disappearing from the cross" rather than submitting to its shame and accepting the insults against Him and His Father. Celsus' conclusion: the message of the cross is indeed foolishness.

Faced with such values in the surrounding culture, the Corinthian Christians apparently began to emphasize the wisdom of God in such a way that it would be more palatable to the Greek way of thinking. Because the cross fit least well into a vision of wisdom focused on beauty, goodness, and rational order, they may well have begun to concentrate rather on eloquent wisdom, spiritual gifts, and wise speech and knowledge *at the expense* of the word of the cross. Conformity to the wisdom of the world around them threatened to empty the cross of its meaning for the Corinthian Christians.

Finally, many of the Christians at Corinth were apparently also fascinated with both spiritual and material power. The city of Corinth boasted not only many philosopher schools, but many religious groups and currents. Each offered its own version of power: power to accomplish the extraordinary, power to open deep religious mysteries, power to ascend to the heights of religious experience. Those who demonstrated special powers also expected and claimed special privileges—easily enough obtainable from the crowds fascinated by the mysterious. Spiritual ratings were prevalent: the spiritual ones distinguished themselves proudly from the less spiritual. And those who exhibited extraordinary spiritual powers simultaneously claimed privileges of higher honor, respect, financial, and social status.

This fascination with spiritual and material power also led to deviations and divisions in the Corinthian congregation. Some considered themselves spiritually superior to others because they could perform extraordinary miracles or speak in unknown tongues. Some criticized the Apostle Paul because his rhetoric was not eloquent and powerful, or because he maintained a humble social and economic status. Some rationalized that their spiritual power and freedom raised them above the petty considerations of faithfulness in marriage. Some discounted the resurrection because they had already attained the "new life." Some had moved up in society and were using the levers of the courts to obtain greater economic status.

This conformity to the power of the world around them threatened to shatter the Corinthian Christians' fellowship and empty the cross of its power. Paul reminded his readers by their own experience and by the heart of the gospel story that God, however, chose what was weak in the world to shame the strong and begged them to return wholeheartedly to "Christ crucified," in deed the power of God. Conformity to the word of the cross would correct the Corinthian Christians' fascination with signs and power as manageable proof of divine intervention and justification of their own spiritual and material status.

3. What Is the "Word of the Cross?"

What is this "word of the cross" which the apostle repeatedly placed before the early Christians? How does "Jesus Christ and him crucified" represent the power and wisdom of God—the kind of wisdom and power which differs radically from the kind prized and promoted by an unbelieving society and culture?

The Apostle Paul reminded his readers that none of the rulers of this age understood the wisdom and power of God in Christ. Had they understood and accepted it rather than desperately trying to preserve their own power and wisdom, "they would not have crucified the Lord of glory" (1 Corinthians 2:8).

Those who crucified Jesus were precisely the ones who stood for the kind of wisdom and power which exercised a tantalizing influence on the Corinthian Christians. The Jewish leaders, preoccupied with signs and manifestations of divine power, clamored for the crucifixion of Him who offered them only the sign of Jonah and entered Jerusalem on a humble donkey instead of a magnificent war horse. The Roman leaders, representing traditional wisdom, political might, and legal power, cross-examined Jesus by pressing for His definition of truth as well as a confession of His complicity in a movement seeking political power. To preserve their synthesis of wisdom and power, they sent Jesus off to be crucified.

In another epistle, Paul used three verbs to express more adequately what happened to these kinds of wisdom and power at the cross. At the cross, God "disarmed" worldly power and wisdom and "made a public example of them," thus "triumphing over them" (Colossians 2:15). In what way did God make a public example of unbelieving wisdom and power at the cross, triumph over them, and disarm them?

It is first of all precisely in the crucifixion that the true nature of unbelieving wisdom and power has come to light. Prior to the cross, they were accepted as basic and ultimate realities of this world, as standards by which to measure human experience and religious endeavor.

Previously people had not perceived that this belief was based upon an illusion. Philosophers had believed that such power enabled the preservation and guaranteed the security of society and individual persons, that such wisdom provided the necessary insight to understand the meaning of life and to solve the riddle of human existence.

But when the one true God appeared on earth in Christ, it became apparent that the highest human wisdom and the greatest human power of the time were His adversaries rather than His instruments. Now the belief in them and the dedication to them is unmasked as deceptive and illusory: they are made a public spectacle.

By unmasking the claims of worldly wisdom and power to be the final arbiters of human experience and piety, God also "triumphs" over them. The unmasking is already their defeat. During the present time, however, only the men and women who know that God Himself has appeared on earth in Jesus Christ can see what has happened. Only those "who are being saved" (1 Corinthians 1:18) hear the word of the cross as a word of genuine power rather than of weakness. To "those who are being lost," the cross appears as weakness on the part of Christ and power on the part of those who ordered His crucifixion. But what Christ already accomplished at the cross became manifest in His resurrection, namely, that in Christ God challenged the best of human wisdom and power, penetrated their territory, and demonstrated that He remains stronger and wiser than they.

The evidence of this triumph is that at the cross Christ also disarmed human power and wisdom in their claims to attain the highest truth and deploy the greatest strength. As Hendrik Berkhof has pointed out, the weapon of this kind of wisdom and power "was the power of illusion, their ability to convince men that they were . . . regents of the world, ultimate certainty and ultimate direction, ultimate happiness and ultimate duty for small, dependent humanity. Since Christ we know that this is an illusion. We are called to a higher destiny: we have higher orders to follow and we stand under a greater protector. . . . Unmasked, revealed in their true nature, they have lost their mighty grip on men. The cross has disarmed them: wherever it is preached, their unmasking and disarming take place."

The word of the cross, therefore, frees "those who are being saved" from the kind of wisdom and power which crucified Christ and opens to them a vision and reality of the alternate power and wisdom manifest in Him. What is the shape of this alternate power and wisdom? And how does conformity to the word of the cross lead to church unity and faithful Christian conduct?

4. The Cross and Servanthood

The power of Christ crucified is the power of servanthood. In Philippians 2:7 the Apostle Paul recounted how Christ Jesus "emptied himself, taking the form of a servant." In his first letter to the Corinthians, the apostle stated that he and Apollos were nothing more than servants. They could make no claims to final authority over the Christians at Corinth. The power which had been given them was the power to execute faithfully the task of building up the body of Christ, not the power to dominate others and acquire an elevated status in the church or in the surrounding society. As servants of Christ they both belonged to *all* the Christians in Corinth, who in turn *all* belonged to Christ, the Servant par excellence.

Paul thus admonished the Corinthian Christians to conform to the word of the cross as it takes the shape of servanthood rather than to a society bent on the acquisition of power as domination. Serving rather than dominating becomes the principle of Christian unity and fellowship; sacrificing rather than the manipulation of personal and material status the path to congregational solidarity. Common subordination to the servanthood of

Jesus Christ, rather than the proud promotion of extraordinary spiritual powers, chart the course to Christian excellence. Seeking to demonstrate the mind of Christ—rather than glorifying individual uniqueness—leads the way to church unity and Christian obedience.

The same may be said of the alternate wisdom rooted in the word of the cross. The wisdom of God in Christ reveals a new creation which transcends and judges the fallen world that unbelieving wisdom seeks to justify. As someone has observed, human rationality at its best still "seeks its foundation and its justification in the forces which hold the world in its eternal order, and which also surround with superior forces the mighty human spirit itself."

The wisdom revealed by the word of the cross, however, does not seek to understand and justify fallen creation apart from Christ and then to fit Christ into the scheme of things so understood. It rather recognizes that the inner structure of the world is transitory. The alternate wisdom of the cross, therefore, begins with the new creation in Christ and understands the world in that light. The alternate wisdom of the cross recognizes that even though the world in its effort to probe the depths of truth and reality rejected Christ, God has revealed in Him the beginning of a new humanity and will make all things one with Himself in Christ (Colossians 1). Conformity to this vision of reality will become visible in a Christian obedience discernible by its resemblance to the cross of Christ rather than by whether it fits well within the acceptable moral standards of an unbelieving society.

Glorify Thy Name

"Father, glorify Thy name. I will not seek my own comfort or deliverance, I simply dare not; but I am willing, in Thy strength, and because I love Thee so, to suffer anything, if only Thy glory may be promoted, so that men may think better of Thee, because of what they see in me." What a battle cry is this—Father, glorify thy name! How it must thrill the hosts of heaven, as they see some dauntless soul descending into death, with these words upon the lips. How it must strike amazement and panic into the hosts of hell! Scaevola held his hand in the flame till it was burnt to ashes, to show the stuff of which Romans were made; and here is the spirit of all God's saints. To ignore the shrinking flesh, to trample it in the dust, to nail it to the cross; to follow the path, clearly pointed by the will of God; to charge into the valley of death, whilst destruction is belched from the cannon's mouth, "here is the patience and the faith of the saints."

—F. B. Meyer in *Gospel of John*.

8

GLORIFY THY NAME

By Martin W. Lehman

Unless a grain of wheat falls into the earth and dies, it remains alone; but if it dies, it bears much fruit. John 12:24. Father, glorify thy name. John 12:28.

A seed is safe if it stays cool and dry and above ground. But a seed's chief reason for being is to bear fruit, which it can do only at great risk to itself. It must fall into warm, moist earth—ideal for bacteria, decay, and death. But warm, moist earth is ideal also for germination, growth, and fruit-bearing.

Long before the earth sprouted vegetation, with plants yielding seed and fruit trees bearing fruit—in fact, before the foundation of the earth was laid—a decision was made, an agreement reached. Father, Son, and Holy Spirit determined that the Seed should fall into the ground.

Jesus was that Seed. If He had not agreed to be the Seed, the Creator's voice would have been silent. But

Martin W. Lehman, Tampa, Florida, has been a pastor and presently serves as bishop among the Florida Mennonite churches.

with His consent, the Creator's voice rang out, "Let there be . . ." and there was.

For millenniums the Son-Seed was safe, but finally the right time came. He came to earth as the God-man. Little is known of Him for thirty years except that He was a good son, a good man, and, we may assume, a good carpenter.

And then for the next 3½ years the Spirit moved Him mightily. He spoke with authority—exposing hypocrisy, confounding critics, forgiving sins. He spoke plainly, and ordinary people liked it.

He fed thousands. He walked on water. He ruled the weather. He cast out evil spirits. He healed all diseases. He raised the dead. The people saw and heard and believed. They crowded around Him, followed Him, and loved Him.

Great waves of popularity swelled about Him. The Jewish multitudes saw in Jesus the fulfillment of their destiny as the chosen people ruled by David's Son in the promised land. They were sure God's Anointed One had come. They wanted to make Him King. He could wait, but they couldn't. They would force a crown on Him. They would make Him King as their fathers had made His father, David, king. David's Son would lead them in battle. With sword and spear, bow and arrow and sling, they'd drive all enemy soldiers from their land. The jubilee of jubilees had come.

More fame awaited Him. "The Greeks wish to see you," reported Andrew and Philip. Yes, the hour had come for Him to be glorified. But what glory! It was not to be the glory of ascending, of a coronation. It was to be the dubious glory of descending, as of a seed falling into the ground.

He Knew the Future

Jesus had long known it would come to this. Six months before, just as it had been revealed to His disciples that He was the Christ, the Son of the living God, He had begun to reveal His destiny. "The son of man must be betrayed, be crucified, die, and be buried, and be raised to life on the third day," He told them. But His disciples didn't believe Him.

But He knew that what He said was true. And it would be soon. Sometimes, He wanted to be alone with His disciples. And again, He seemed to want to attract to Himself the public attention of the whole land. He moved back and forth across the country explaining with more power and beauty than ever before the nature of the kingdom. He called Himself the Light of the World and the Good Shepherd of God's flock.

Perhaps He was troubled by the contrast between what He had promised to do and the other alternative before Him. Only a nod of His head and the people would crown Him King. Only a beck of His finger and twelve legions of angels would quickly rid the land of every Roman soldier in a six-minute blitz. In no time at all from His throne He could command worldwide righteousness. But what glory is there in a righteousness compelled by law?

Perhaps He was troubled by the knowledge of what following Him would bring on His disciples. Always He had been fair with would-be disciples. "Birds have nests and foxes have dens," He'd told them, "but I have no place of My own to lay My head. You must deny yourself and take up your cross, if you follow Me." He knew that because of Him husbands and wives would separate, parents and children would be at odds. He knew that if the world hated, rejected, and killed Him it would hate, reject, and kill His followers. Must He bring them to that? Could He not let them compromise with the world, let them take the hand from the plow? But what glory is there in being a leader with no followers?

Perhaps He was troubled by all of these—by the nearness of the event, the injustice about to be done to Him, by the contrast between what was to be and what might be, and by what He was about to bring on His followers. The weight was too much to bear. Perhaps He could pray, "Father, save me from this hour"! Perhaps He could simply ascend and let the Father justly rain fire and brimstone on the earth, a fate which befell Sodom and Gomorrah. But what glory would failure bring to the Father?

As His popularity peaked, the opposition hardened. The rulers of the Jews, threatened by what He said and did and by the kind of man He was, determined to get rid of Him. Knowing that the Seed sowing time was near, He turned toward Jerusalem. "Don't go," His disciples warned Him. They'll kill You there."

"You're right," He assured them. "A prophet should be killed nowhere but in Jerusalem." Calmly, He faced toward Jerusalem.

"Now Is My Soul Troubled"

But now in Jerusalem, during His last public discourse, the calm cracked. "My soul is troubled," He confessed. He who once rebuked His disciples with, "Why are you troubled?" and who later comforted them with "Let not your heart be troubled," was now Himself troubled— disturbed, agitated, distressed.

Why was He troubled? Perhaps in His humanity, He

momentarily rebelled against keeping a commitment made eons ago in a heaven where pain and death were unreal. As the hour neared, He may have asked, as we all do at times: How did I get into this? Is this fair? Am I trapped? Can I be released from my commitment? But what glory is in evasion of duty, in breaking one's word?

Perhaps He was troubled by the injustice about to be done to Him. As God's blessing incarnate, He had brought joy to cripples, tax collectors, children, and prostitutes. Now He who lifted up so many must Himself be brought low. As God's holiness incarnate, He had loved sinners and forgiven them their sins. Now He who was the only Man ever to have kept Himself pure must Himself bear every man's sin. As the incarnate love of God, He must be hated. He who had never shed another's blood must allow His own blood to be shed. Why must He become a public curse—ridiculed, blasphemed? But then what glory is there in naked justice?

No, He could not be saved from this hour. In truth, He had come for this hour. The promise of this hour had allowed creation to begin, spared the earth when Adam fell, saved Noah and his family from the flood. The hour had been anticipated by the sacrifices of the law of Moses and had been announced by all the prophets. He was the only hope. The Seed must fall.

Like a trapeze artist who in midair lets go the bar, so the Son relaxed His grip on the power and the glory of diety to plunge to earth. On earth He must now let go of physical life and give His corpse to the earth.

"Glorify Thy Name"

Faced with His ultimate duty, its prospect and its promise, and with new resolve to fulfill His destiny, calm returned. But only for a moment. It gave way to excitement, exultation. "Father," he cried, "glorify thy name."

"I have glorified it, and I will glorify it again," the Father thundered in reply. Father and Son rejoiced in that glory.

Father and Son gloried in His dying. They knew that for three hours the earth would be dark and still. Then the earth would quake, rocks would break, the graves would open. Men and women would cry out in fear and beat their breasts as the Father proclaimed in a voice too loud for man to hear, "This is my beloved Son, with whom I am well pleased." Too late they would acknowledge His innocence; too late they would confess His diety. The glory was terrifying.

Father and Son gloried in the Lamb of God. They knew that though the searing pain of crucifixion raced through His body, though He thirsted, though He felt forsaken by His God, He would not curse. He would give His wounded mother to His beloved disciple. He would forgive the soldiers gambling at His feet. He would comfort the dying thief with hope. He would trust His Spirit to the Father, and die willingly, gladly. For by dying the Lamb would purchase life for all who believed. By accepting death's sting, He would remove it. By allowing His flesh to be torn, He would rend the veil in the temple. By surrendering His body to His foe, He would defeat him. By being lifted up, He would draw all people to Himself. The Lamb would prove perfect.

Father and Son gloried in the resurrection. They knew it would be impossible to keep His body in the tomb. On the morning of the third day, to the surprise of His disciples and the dismay of His enemies, the tomb would break open, the Seed would burst forth. And by the power of the resurrection men and women would live abundantly. The resurrected Seed would be the first fruit of them that slept.

Father and Son gloried in the fruit the Seed would bear. The fruit would be His sons and daughters. They would bear the image of the Father, exhibit His character, share His work, and His inheritance. The fruit would be saints. As the temples of the Holy Spirit, they would cleanse themselves of the filth of the flesh to become pure as He is pure. The fruit would be *martyrs,* bearing in their bodies the dying of Jesus. They would fall seedlike into the ground. The fruit would be abundant.

Father and Son gloried in the kingdom of God. They knew that the *citizens* of the kingdom would have the right to immediate personal audience with the King. The *soldiers* of the kingdom would refuse all weapons which cripple, kill, and destroy. Instead, they would fight with the Word of God, which, when used in faith and accompanied by prayer, could deal with the real enemies, the wicked spirits in places of authority. The *ambassadors* of the kingdom would make true peace, reconciling God and man, and man with man, through the gospel. The *town meeting* of the kingdom would be the church, gathered to worship the King, to discern His will, and to plan to carry it out. The kingdom would be eternal.

Father and Son gloried in the future restoration of all things. They knew that the earth, now groaning in birth pain and waiting impatiently for the manifestation of the sons of God, would not pass away before coming into its own. In that apocalyptic day Satan would be cast out. Judgment would free the earth of its curse. The trees would clap their hands, the lion and the lamb would lie down together. Every man would rest in the shelter of his own vine and fig tree. The nations would study war no more. The King of kings would come. The hope of the ages would be fulfilled.

Father and Son gloried in the eternal glory. They knew that out of every age and from every nation, kindred, tribe, and tongue would come the saints. Clothed in robes washed in the blood of the Lamb, they would cast their crowns at His feet. Never again would there be sorrow or tears, pain or death. The Son-Seed and His fruit would be together throughout eternity.

No wonder the calm gave way to exultation. They knew that the joy before Him would sustain Him in His appointed hour. He was ready to fall into the ground; it could not keep Him; He could not abide alone; He would bear much fruit. He and his seed would be the glory of His Father. Amen.

The Word of Forgiveness

The seven sayings on the cross are seven windows through which we can see into the soul of our Savior. Words are like lightening flashes through which we see the Speaker's thoughts. Three utterances were spoken to God and four to mankind.

Seven times He spoke, seven words of love,
And all three hours, His silence cried
For mercy on the souls of men;
Jesus, our Lord, is crucified.

—Author unknown

9
THE WORD OF FORGIVENESS
By James M. Lapp

And Jesus said, "Father, forgive them; for they know not what they do." Luke 23:34.

Out of the revolution in Zaire (formerly the Congo) comes the story of Joseph W. Tucker, an American missionary from the Ozark mountains of Arkansas. During twenty-five years of service in the Congo, Tucker had developed a great proficiency in the native languages and translated many books into Swahili. Twenty schools, including one college, were established through his help. During the summer of 1964 when increasing outbreaks of violence were occurring in the Congo, Joe Tucker and his family returned from a furlough in America to their place of service, against the counsel of their friends.

Within a few weeks of their return their village was captured by the rebels and they were seized along with other missionaries. On the day before Thanksgiving, as

---

James M. Lapp, pastor of the Albany (Ore.) Mennonite Church has taken special training in marriage and family counseling. Earlier he served as a pas- in Pennsylvania.

rescue forces neared their village, Mr. Tucker was dragged from his place of confinement and beaten to death. According to witnesses to his execution, it was not a quick and merciful death. The beating took forty-five minutes, one blow at a time, with each new blow only falling after his groaning from the previous blow had ceased.

When reporters spoke to Mrs. Tucker after the rescue of her and her children, the only comment she had was, "I understand why these things happen."

Louis Cassels, the UPI writer who reported this story, commented, "In that simple, compassionate sentence you can hear quite clearly the echo of another voice speaking from the cross: 'Father, forgive them; for they know not what they do.' "

Amidst the unfolding drama of the early church comes the brief story of Stephen. This servant of God, "full of grace and power," astounded the people of Jerusalem with his signs and wonders. So threatening was this man to the established religious order that covert attempts were made to discredit him, and with trumped up charges he was publicly condemned. The power of his testimony on the witness stand was more than the religious authorities could take. Perhaps goaded on by a heckler, Stephen cried out, "You stiff-necked people, uncircumcised in heart and ears, you always resist the Holy Spirit" (Acts 7:51). Was this a cry of bitter malice at those falsely accusing him?

As his critics ground their teeth in uncontrollable rage, Stephen was granted a momentary vision of the heavenly court, with the living Christ standing at the Father's right hand. As the stones began to fly and breath was fleeting from him, Stephen "knelt down and cried with a loud voice, "'Lord, do not hold this sin against them' " (Acts 7:60).

From where does this spirit of forgiveness in the lives of those unjustly suffering death arise? Luke 23 presents to us just such a spirit being modeled in the life of our Lord in His own death.

1. The Scene

These simple words, "Father, forgive them," did not originate from a pious pulpiteer admonishing a congregation, or a doting grandparent supervising children in their play. These words come from the lips of a Man who called no person His enemy and was known near and far for His acts of compassion and love. Now He hung naked and bleeding from a Roman cross.

The scene where these words were first uttered was called Golgotha, meaning "skull," located not too far from a well-traveled Judean road (Mark 15:22). Possibly a hill just outside the city of Jerusalem was chosen so the violent deeds done there could be safely observed from a distance (Mark 15:40). According to the early church father, Jerome, skulls cluttered this hillside as mute evidence of the ruthless business performed here.

Crucifixion was among the cruelest of deaths. Not to be discounted is the brutal pain of the terrible process itself. Even more dreaded was the terror of being left to die of hunger and thirst as the hot Palestinian days and cool nights came and went. William Barclay says, "Many a criminal was known to have hung for a week upon his cross until he died raving mad."

This is the scene from which we receive this word of forgiveness. At the feet of our Lord men gambled for His clothing. To His sides hung two men cursing in fitful anger as the sharp pains of their wounds ravished their bodies. Off a little ways were the weeping women and friends. Already Jesus had spent a sleepless night being pushed and shoved from courtroom to courtroom in Jerusalem. Now in weariness and brokenness rough nails held His body to the cross.

More than likely these same soldiers had come to Golgotha many times. Common to their ears were the curses and outcries of the criminal executed here. But this day something was different. For from the middle cross, instead of cursing came a prayer—a prayer of forgiveness from a supposed criminal for His executioners.

2. *The Prayer*

Now perhaps a prayer would not be startling to hear from the lips of a dying man. Many a person will instinctively pray when the chips are down and there seems no other direction to turn than to God. But what is the usual content of such emergency prayers? Perhaps a cry for vengeance on one's enemies, a plea for relief from pain, a quick promise to do anything if only the tragedy is averted, or possibly such a person might even pray for a speedy death and escape from prolonged suffering.

But the first word of Jesus on the cross was none of these. It was rather a prayer of *compassion,* "Father, forgive them." Jesus' prayer was for others, especially those who had contributed to His suffering. Who might Jesus have had in mind in this prayer? Perhaps it was Peter and the other disciples who fled that night, breaking their vows of loyalty and devotion to the Master. Maybe Jesus was thinking of Pilate, that cowardly governor of Judea; or of Herod, the contemptible king of Galilee; or possibly of sneering Caiaphas, the high priest. Most likely flashes of Judas' face and that memorable cold kiss taunted Jesus in His weakened condition, and this prayer was for him. Surely the soldiers who mocked as they pounded the nails and now bartered for His garments were included in this prayer of compassion by our Lord. But how about you and me and the rest of mankind whose sins caused the Son of God to be executed? Might not we also be included in this intercessory prayer of forgiveness by Jesus?

This was also a prayer of *confession* on the part of Jesus. Here was a confession of pain, of suffering, of shame, of loneliness, of need. How often Jesus' followers today want to gloss over the hurts of life which they receive. "It's okay," biting our lips lest anyone discover our distress. Not Jesus. He knew forgiveness of others does not demand denial of the hurt we have received at their hands.

Here too was a prayer of *confrontation.* "Forgive them; for they know not what they do." He confronted them in their ignorance, called attention to their hypocrisy, challenged their philosophy of "I'm only taking orders" as a valid basis for behavior. Forgiveness is not a cheap gift. It causes others to face up to their misdeeds even when they claim innocence. Jesus might have prayed in silence for those involved in His crucifixion. But forgiveness does not mean the abusers escape the gravity of their actions or responsibility for their misdeeds. By an open prayer of intercession Jesus caused His executioners to face up to their sin.

3. *The Example*

The crowds had heard Jesus teach His disciples some months earlier how to respond to those who unjustly accuse you and harm you. "If any one strikes you on the right cheek, turn to him the other also" he had boldly said (Matthew 5:39). Now they had an opportunity to see if He really meant it. "Love your enemies," he commanded His disciples "and pray for those who persecute you" (Matthew 5:44). Did He really mean this? Here was the public test of whether or not these were the fanciful words of an idealist, or in fact a practical way of living. "For if you forgive men their trespasses, your heavenly Father also will forgive you; but if you do not forgive men their trespasses, neither will your Father forgive your trespasses" (Matthew 6:14, 15). Such words were not hollow advice, for on the cross the Son of Man demonstrated this very spirit par excellence.

It is one thing for a teacher or preacher to promulgate great lofty ideals of human behavior. It is quite another thing to ask whether or not he lives by these noble teachings in his own life. We might have basis for some neat realizations or for searching for loopholes in these hard texts, if it wasn't for the fact that Jesus so perfectly modeled in His own life and death the very ideals He set forth regarding treatment of those who abuse us. He demonstrated a powerful new alternative in human relationships, an honest prayer of compassionate, confrontive love and forgiveness in the face of suffering and death.

Jesus the Teacher now becomes Jesus the Example in one of the most difficult aspects of His teaching. Contrary to some interpretations, this is not passive absorbing of hurt in weakness, but tough love expressed in the positive strength of true forgiveness.

4. The Calling

Peter, who likely relived this scene and this prayer of Jesus a thousand times wrote so appropriately in his first letter, "For Christ suffered for you and left you a personal example, and wants you to follow in his steps. . . . When he was insulted he offered no insult in return. When he suffered he made no threats of revenge" (1 Peter 2:21, 23; Phillips). There were no threats of revenge from Him who had at His disposal twelve legions of angels (Matthew 26:53), but rather an intercessory prayer of forgiveness.

This first word from the cross is a call to God's people in every generation to live a genuine life of forgiving love to others. Paul states it very pointedly in his letter to the Ephesians: " . . . be kind to one another, tenderhearted, forgiving one another, as God in Christ forgave you" (Ephesians 4:32). The model of God's forgiveness of us in Christ as He hung on the cross is to become our pattern for living with each other.

One day as a husband described to me the sad current events from his homelife, and the disappointment and discouragement of his marriage, I quietly asked him, "What would it take to forgive her, John?" His response was simply, "I don't know. That's one of my hardest areas."

Forgiveness is a hard thing to do, not only from a cross in the face of your tormenters, but in the home with a spouse or children who have let you down, in the church, in society, on the job, or wherever it may be that hurt is experienced. Forgiveness is never easy.

A divorced woman once shared with me the cruelty and pain surrounding the dissolution of her marriage. For many years she harbored malice and bitterness in her heart toward her former spouse and those involved in the nasty affair. The evidence of her mistreatment was readily available on tape and in writing. She wanted to move on in her life in Christ, but these experiences continued to rankle inside her. One day while reading the story of Corrie ten Boom, she found courage to take all the old evidence she had been hoarding and destroy it. For her it was a beautiful day of liberation. Forgiveness in the face of hurt brings healing and wholeness of life.

An unforgiving spirit of bitterness does more harm to the one harboring it than to the person toward whom it is directed. To refuse to forgive is to become a victim of the sins and misdeeds of others, and of our own tendencies toward self-pity. From the cross, our Lord offers us the positive choice of forgiveness which can bring release of spirit and wholeness within and open the way to healing our relationships with others.

Instead of the cross of Jesus being a stage for shouting vengeance, it became a platform for proclaiming forgiveness. That's usually where forgiveness needs to be expressed, from a cross or some other place of hurt. But he who found the grace to pray, "Father, forgive," while experiencing the throes of death can enable us to so live and pray and forgive in our most difficult circumstances of life.

The Word of Pardon

Josephine Robertson, in her book *Living with Love*, tells this story:

In 1883 a youthful clergyman, Joe Roberts, arrived by stage-coach in a blizzard to minister to the Indians of Wyoming. This great, wild area had been assigned to the Protestant Episcopal Church by President Grant. Soon after Joe Roberts arrived, the son of the chief was shot by a soldier in a brawl, and Chief Washakie vowed to kill the first white man he met. Since this might mean the start of a long, bloody feud, young Roberts decided to take action. Seeking out the tepee, fifteen miles away in the mountains, he stood outside and called the chief's name. When Washakie appeared, Roberts opened his shirt.

"I have heard of your vow," he said. "I know that the other white men have families, but I am alone. Kill me instead."

The chief was amazed and motioned him into his tent. "How do you have so much courage?" he asked.

Joe Roberts told him about Christ, His death, His teachings. They talked for hours. When Joe left, the chief of the Shoshones had renounced his vow to kill and had resolved to become a Christian.

Washakie had seen the love of the cross in action.

10

THE WORD OF PARDON

By Janet H. Kreider

And he said to him, "Truly, I say to you, today you will be with me in Paradise." Luke 23:43.

The Man on the center cross was quiet now.

The crowd jeered.

The soldiers at His feet looked up, mocking.

"Forgive them," He had said. "They don't know what they are doing." And then He was quiet again.

The crowd surged forward for a better look.

"King of the Jews!" someone shrilled. "Some king!"

The men on the outer crosses writhed in agony. How could He be so still?

The one on the left joined in the jeering, scoffing, and covering Him with abuse. "Why don't you save yourself?" he taunted. "If you're a king, prove it."

(It felt good to be part of the crowd, one with those who hurled insults.)

Janet H. Kreider, East Petersburg, Pennsylvania, has been active in editorial work since 1957. She is assistant editor of *Missionary Messenger* and editor of *Threads of Truth*, a monthly newssheet of women's activities.

"And save us, too, while you're about it."

What blasphemy! Elevating himself to the level of Jesus, the first thief claimed His help, while his heart was hardened against Him.

"There would have been help for the robber and murderer," says F. W. Krummacher in *The Suffering Saviour*, "but there is no deliverance for the impenitent scoffer and hardened child of unbelief."

But the second thief checked the first.

"Don't you even fear God," he asked, "the One we soon must face? For we have sinned and we deserve to die. But this Man—"

And he lifted his eyes to the thorn-torn King with the sign above His head.

Had he seen Him before when He healed the sick?

Or when He gave sight to blind eyes?

Perhaps he had been one of the five thousand who ate from the small boy's lunch.

Or was he a friend of Judas, who also loved money?

Or had he merely heard Him pray, and knew that He knew God?

"This Man has done no wrong," he said. "We are receiving justice, but this Man *is* a King."

"Here is divine illumination in midnight darkness," says Krummacher. "Even the enlightenment of an apostle scarcely reaches to this malefactor's height of faith. 'Lord,' he says, not rabbi, not teacher, or master; no, in the word 'Kyrie' he applies to Him the title of Majesty."

"Lord, remember me when you come into your kingdom."

And as the Man on the center cross opened His eyes, the hill became a throne room as the Judge of all the world extended pardon. "Verily I say to you," He said, "this very day you will be with Me in Paradise."

He had asked only to be remembered,

But Jesus gave, as He always does, abundantly above all asked or thought. "You will be *with* Me, not only in My thoughts, but in My presence." The pardon included the promise of His presence in Paradise. "We have sinned," the thief had said, "and we deserve to die." But Jesus said, "Today . . . with Me . . . in Paradise. Today! At once! Not fifty years from now—Not when I come again to claim My own—But now—today!"

He found forgiveness for his troubled past, peace for the painful present, and hope for the unknown future.

Jesus clothed the naked, dying thief with His robe of righteousness so he could enter in.

> Three men hung on three crosses that day;
> On each side a sinner; in the center, the Way.
> One criminal taunted, the other believed;
> The first one rejected, the second received.
> "If you are God, prove it"—"Remember me, Lord."
> To the scoffer the Way had no promising word;
> To the other, with love-mingled-pain in His eyes,
> "Together—today—you and I—Paradise!"

1. Pardon

The story of the repentant thief on the cross means more than hope for a deathbed conversion. It shows the ever-present response of the Son of God to a questing heart. As the sufferer called out to the Suffering King, he was met at his point of need.

The first thief wanted salvation from his cross; the second wanted salvation for himself.

134 The Way of the Cross and Resurrection

He did not ask directly for forgiveness, although he had admitted he had sinned. Jesus had heard his confession to the mocking thief. He had asked only to be remembered, but Jesus' response assured him that he had received a pardon.

One is pardoned when he is freed from the penalty due for an offense. One pardons when he refrains from exacting punishment that is deserved. Pardon denotes a release, not from guilt, but from penalty.

Larry Lehman, missionary in Guatemala, tells of a man from Chitana who is so strong he can carry a huge beam on his shoulder as if it were a piece of firewood. Many people feared him because of his great strength.

One day this strong man was led to the Lord by a frightened but dedicated brother who discovered that he was hungry for the Word of God. Soon after he believed, however, his cow died mysteriously, then a pig and a dog. The man and his family were ostracized by the community. Even their lives were threatened.

But these trials only drew the man from Chitana nearer to the Lord. God removed hate and anger from his heart and filled him with love for his neighbors. Less than two years later there were 35 people in the community who believed, some of them the same persons who had earlier rejected him for his faith.

But fifteen men who were angered by this turn of events plotted to destroy the man from Chitana. They drew up a paper under oath saying that he had removed images from the local church and burned them. When the man was brought before the authorities, however, he was quickly acquitted.

The judge then wanted to prosecute the accusers for perjury, but the man from Chitana, who for years had fought with his great strength any who had threatened him, pleaded with the judge for their pardon. The judge granted his request, and within a year the community of believers grew to 135.

During Revolutionary War days, Peter Miller, a minister in the Bethany Reformed Church in Ephrata, withdrew from his church and joined the Seventh-Day Baptists. This transfer incurred the wrath of Michael Witman, a deacon of the church Peter had left. Witman tried his best to make life miserable for Peter; on one occasion he slapped him in the face and on another he spit on him. But Peter never returned the abuse in any way.

Some time later Witman expressed his views in favor of the British. Overheard by American spies, he was arrested, tried for treason, and sentenced to be hanged.

When Peter, who was a personal acquaintance of General George Washington, heard of Witman's sentence, he walked through the snow for sixty miles from Ephrata to Valley Forge to intercede for Witman's life. General Washington told him his request for his friend could not be granted, but Peter said, "My friend! I haven't a worse enemy living than that man!"

That any man would walk sixty miles to save his enemy so impressed General Washington that he granted Witman's pardon.

Peter then trudged fifteen more miles to West Chester where the execution was to take place. Witman, being carried to the scaffold as Peter arrived, chided him for coming to see his revenge gratified. But Peter in reply waved the pardon and the doomed man was set free.

Witman was pardoned, not from his guilt, but from the penalty by the authority of the word of General Washington.

The repentant thief was pardoned from eternal death by the only One who had the authority to grant pardon in the Father's name.

Inspired by the request of the repentant thief, Synesius of Cyrene wrote about AD 410:

> Lord Jesus, think on me,
> And purge away my sin;
> From earthborn passions set me free,
> And make me pure within.
>
> Lord Jesus, think on me,
> With care and woe oppressed;
> Let me Thy loving servant be,
> And taste Thy promised rest.
>
> Lord Jesus, think on me,
> That, when the flood is past,
> I may th'eternal brightness see,
> And share Thy joy at last.

2. Promise

The pardon was in the form of a promise—to be fulfilled immediately. And this promise sustained the man—when the darkness came, when the earth shook beneath him, when the soldiers came to break his legs. This man to whom he had entrusted his life would not make an empty promise.

An elderly saint was deeply disturbed because he could no longer remember verses of the Bible he had memorized in his youth. A young minister who visited him found him in tears. "For years I had been memorizing the promises of the Word of God," the elderly man said. "I thought when I came to my last hours I could repeat them and find comfort in them, but my memory has failed me and I can recall only snatches."

Quick as a flash the young minister said, "But God has not forgotten them. Just rest in the Promiser Himself."

The word of the Promiser was to be fulfilled that day.

"Where is he now?" This is the question Natasha asks at the deathbed of her lover Prince Andre in Tolstoy's *War and Peace*. And it is the universal question the grieving ask the moment the breath of a loved one stops and the body, the form which they had known and loved and whose warm touch brought pleasure, turns cold and still. "Where is he now?"

To the Christian this promise brings comfort. He is with the Lord, and the world of the spirit may be closer than we think.

Describing the death of his wife of fifty-five years, Cornelius Wall said, "Peace settled on her face as she drew her last breath. It was a step she had to take alone. . . . The step out of time into eternity, out of our companionship into the presence of our Savior" (*Christian Leader*, May 11, 1976).

What did the first thief think about when the railing crowd had scattered and he was left to die alone beside the God he had mocked? He had no promise or Promiser to rest in.

3. Presence

The promise included being in the presence of Jesus, wherever He was.

When we love someone, it is good to know they think about us when we are separated. We look eagerly for letters or listen for a telephone call. But how much more satisfying to be *with* them.

When my brother and his family went to Israel as

missionaries in 1953, we eagerly waited for letters. How good it was to hear from them about the land where Jesus had lived and to read about the growing-up experiences of their children. But how much better it was to visit them fifteen years later, to walk the streets where Jesus walked, to be *with* them as they told us about their life there.

The presence of a loved visitor at the bedside of one who is ill, even when no words are spoken, is comforting and refreshing. Sister Miriam Theresa Winter wrote in a song about "the joy when a loved one enters the room." Conversely, a room filled with people seems empty when a loved person is missing. Cornelius Wall, referred to earlier, said on the death of his wife, "And suddenly I stood there alone! Yes, alone, although I was surrounded by our children and grandchildren."

God promised Moses that His presence would go with him and give him rest. Jesus promised the dying thief that his rest would be in the presence of Jesus in Paradise.

This is the only time Jesus speaks of Paradise. This is Paradise regained, the Paradise of perfect communion with God which was lost when Adam fell.

Jesus made this promise on the eve of His triumph as He was about to overthrow the powers of death and hell. His word was immutable, based on His work of atonement. And the thief was going to be with Him, not because he had earned a reward, but because he had laid hold on God's love by faith.

Jesus' promise to the dying thief has encouraged countless martyrs who could see on the other side of the flames, the rack, and the dark prisons the unending life in His presence.

But more than an unfulfilled promise of some future era is the awareness that the presence of the Holy Spirit indwells each believer, and each day can be lived in His presence so that death is merely a lifting of the veil when we see Him face-to-face.

And now he knows . . .
Here all is darkness.
We hear and wonder,
Is it a Voice
Or is it thunder?
For him the portal
To all things mortal
Has opened
And closed.
He knows.

The Word of Human Care

One of the most profound commentaries ever written on the atonement is the song penned by Cecil Frances Alexander around 1848.

There is a green hill far away,
Outside a city wall,
Where the dear Lord was crucified,
Who died to save us all.

We may not know, we cannot tell
What pains He had to bear;
But we believe it was for us
He hung and suffered there.

He died that we might be forgiv'n,
He died to make us good,
That we might go at last to heav'n,
Saved by His precious blood.

There was no other good enough
To pay the price of sin;
He only could unlock the gate
Of heav'n and let us in.

O dearly, dearly has He loved,
And we must love Him too,
And trust in His redeeming blood,
And try His works to do.

11

THE WORD OF HUMAN CARE

By Emma Richards

When Jesus saw his mother, and the disciple whom he loved standing near, he said to his mother, "Woman, behold, your son!" Then he said to the disciple, "Behold, your mother!" John 19:26, 27.

Sybil was a quiet, gentle Christian who taught school in the same building as I. We had little occasion to talk together except on a professional level. However, one day she stood at my classroom door at the close of the school day and started talking. "Mrs. Richards, I just want to say 'Thank you' to your church. My mother is dying of cancer and her Christian faith stems from your church." Surprised, I asked to hear her story.

"My mother grew up on the near south side of Chicago," she said. "Her home was full of all kinds of unhappiness and problems. My grandfather was a heavy drinker and lived with the family only on occasion. My

---

Emma Richards, Lombard, Illinois, is a public schoolteacher and copastor of the Lombard Mennonite Church. Earlier she served as a missionary in Japan.

grandmother grew bitter and resented the burden of her daughter. So my mother played in the streets and led a lonely, undisciplined, unhappy life.

"One day a lady on the sidewalk invited her to church and out of boredom my mother went. Through this contact my mother became what was called a fresh-air child. Each summer for four years she went to live with the same Mennonite farm family in Indiana. Here she was shown love, was taught how to work, and was expected to share in the total life of the family. My mother was introduced to another side of life. Things didn't have to be like she knew them on the sidewalks of Chicago and in the dingy apartment where she lived.

"To make a long story short, my mother became a Christian and made her life decisions on the basis of that commitment. The farm parents who cared for her over fifty years ago are gone, and the Home Mission is gone, torn down to make way for the expressway. But my mother's faith is alive and well. As I care for her and listen to her story, I am so grateful to the Christians who cared!"

The drama of this incident is new and exciting; however, its message is as old as the Christian faith. Christians are people who care. On the day of crucifixion as Jesus was led out of the city of Jerusalem to that barren skull-shaped hill, a caring drama unfolded. Although the intent of the Gospel writers was to share the drama on the cross, they did not overlook the drama at the foot of the cross.

In that milling, thrill-seeking crowd stood some true friends and followers of Jesus. Who were they? According to Matthew 27:55 "there were also many women there, looking on from afar. . . . Mary Magdalene, and

Mary the mother of James and Joseph, and the mother of the sons of Zebedee." Mark 15:40 says, "There were also women looking on from afar, among whom were Mary Magdalene, and Mary the mother of James the younger and of Joses, and Salome." Luke writes in his Gospel, "And all his acquaintances and the women who had followed him from Galilee stood at a distance and saw these things." And John 19:25 lists "his mother, and his mother's sister, Mary the wife of Clopas, and Mary Magdalene . . . and the disciple whom he loved."

These friends of Jesus could do little. They stood and they looked, but they were there. They cared. They were stricken with their own personal grief. As a mother, an aunt, a cousin, and dear friends, they experienced their own fears and sorrows. They were timid, but felt the need to be bold and brave. They were experiencing the frustrations of their own inadequacy. They could have easily talked themselves out of going there! Listen to them!

Salome, the overprotective mother of James and John: "I wonder if I should be here. My presence might make it hard for James and John. I'm really not doing much but standing here. Perhaps I should be home cooking and caring for my husband and sons. Isn't that where all good mothers and wives are to be? Besides, I don't like crowds!"

Jesus' aunt: "I'm not sure why I'm here. Doing my family duty, I suppose. But I'm a bother rather than a help. I feel faint and this whole thing is such a puzzle to me. Perhaps I should be home really crying and getting my emotions out so that I'm ready to help the family work through their grief."

John: "This situation calls for leadership and decisive

action. Peter should really be here. He'd know exactly what to say and do. Perhaps if I wouldn't have come, he would have. Then things would be different and we'd see some action. All I can do is stand here with my arm around his mother and cry."

They and the others could have talked and reasoned things. But they were there. They were there because they loved and cared! Their friendship and relationship to Jesus made them persons who were free to love. So it was that Jesus saw His friends near Him in His final hours of suffering.

Out of deep human love Jesus turned to His mother and in simple brevity said, "Woman, look, this is now your son." Jesus provided for His mother. John was to assume the role of elder son. Then Jesus turned to John and in equal brevity he gave the counterpart to his previous statement, "Look, this is now your mother." Willingly John accepted this request and took Mary into his home. Jesus saw and experienced this love and caring before He said, "It is finished."

In the Christian tradition, vocabulary words such as discipleship, brotherhood, community, and fellowship are much used words. Christian commitment calls the believer to a life where these words become real action words. But how does it happen? Has God given the Christian a magic formula? Perhaps not, but the Bible is full of guidelines and illustrations. How do Christians grow and become the effective caring community?

1. Willingness

First of all, one must have a strong desire and willingness to become a caring person. True caring is a result of a Christ-centered committed life. Out of the experience of the new birth should come the desire to care for others. Basic to the Christian's life of action is his faith and knowledge of the Bible. So to truly care for others in a Christlike way, the twentieth-century Christian needs to study the Bible and let the life of Jesus saturate his life.

As this happens the Christian then needs to be willing and consciously wish to become a caring person. He needs to identify with those who share his faith and his desires for service. The church then becomes the base where decisions are made, needs are shared, joys are related, fears and failures are expressed, and commitment deepened.

2. Compassion

The second step toward becoming the caring people of God is compassion. Much of our society is geared toward selfish and self-centered goals for living. Compassion for many is called naivete. Recently one of our large city newspapers carried a front-page story of a sick plant being flown to that city, picked up by ambulance at the airport, and rushed to the office of a horticulturist for diagnosis and treatment.

This event illustrates the cluttered lives of many persons in our society. Although the care of plants is a worthy thing, it must be balanced with the care one has for people. Compassion is learned. It is cultivated. The Christian who walks Calcutta's streets with great compassion serving its people does so because she has not become hardened to need or those in need. Feeling where others are and standing in their shoes is a good thing to do if compassion is to be developed.

One day Jesus sought solitude in a boat after He heard of the death of John the Baptist. But the crowds followed

Him and so He went ashore to be near them. Here "he had compassion on them, and healed their sick" (Matthew 14:14). On another occasion Jesus said, "I'm going to feed these people. They've been with Me three days without food. I have compassion on them" (Matthew 15:32). The life of Jesus was one of compassion—He healed, He taught, and He fed because He had compassion.

3. *Innovation*

The third step toward becoming a caring person is to be free to be innovative. How can I help others? How can we care for each other? Old ways may not provide the answers. Recently I received an original painting from a friend of mine. She wrote of her painting as an act of worship and an avenue of service. But I detected in her letter a note of despair—a church that was not using her gifts. In further correspondence, I learned more about her feelings. My main reaction was that in such a church where I know good leadership resided, how could they be so uncreative? Innovative people are needed in the fellowship of those who care.

4. *Flexibility*

Another thing needed in the caring fellowship are those who are flexible. Caring can become regimented, proper, done within rigid standards, and official minutes. It need not always be so. Caring should also be spontaneous, indigenous, and natural. Keep preoccupied with people not procedure. Jesus did this and was misinterpreted, and some sought to change Him. Others tried to destroy Him. But when the good of others is one's concern, then procedure finds its place among the lesser things. Being flexible does not mean chaos. A Japanese symbol, the bamboo tree, conveys the meaning of flexibility. I recall as a young person standing by the sliding doors of our home in Japan and watching the typhoon winds batter the bamboo grove. When the storm was over the trees stood tall and straight. They adjusted to the need of the hour! So must Christians be willing to bend in the care of others.

5. *Imagination*

If one wishes to be a caring person, he must be willing to use his imagination. Some people in our church were lamenting the commercialization of Christmas. If we really cared about people, how would we share the message of the birth of Christ? Imaginations went to work, and we now have as a major evangelistic thrust in our community a live nativity scene at Christmastime. Families of the church stand in for fifteen minute intervals as Mary, Joseph, and the shepherds. The front porch of the church is converted into the stable. The manger, straw, live sheep, and a live donkey complete the scene. As the caroling fills the air, the people of this suburban community stop to look, listen, and ask questions. The creative imaginations of a few have used the gifts of many persons in our church, and thousands of persons have heard and seen the Christmas message.

6. *Use of Resources*

The caring person is one who is resourceful and willing to use his resources in the care of others. One such resourceful person near the crucifixion scene was Joseph of Arimathea. He was a member of the Sanhedrin who had not voted to condemn Jesus. Perhaps he was a secret disciple. He was a man of wealth, but his main resource on that day was a tomb. And to that tomb, with Pilate's permission, he and Nicodemus carried the body of Jesus and buried it according to the regular Jewish practice.

The caring Christian uses his material resources in the care of others. This is not easy to do in a society that has placed high priority on the amount of material things one can accumulate. Often it is not easy to do in the church where society's standards are all too evident. Big industrial, political, military, and social plans dominate the scene of human events. Does the caring Christian make any difference? In bold headlines, perhaps not, but in the area of human need, yes, people are still loved and made whole.

7. *Trustfulness*

Last of all, the caring Christian must trust God for any results. Too often the Christian is concerned about the results of his caring. Did the family whose burned barn was rebuilt join the church, or did the divorcée see the error of her ways, or will the political system be influenced because of our relief program? As the Holy Spirit guides the Christian in his care of others, so will the Spirit work in the lives of those who have received Christian love and care. Remember, it is God who gives the increase (1 Corinthians 3:6).

Artists have often painted the foot of the cross high above the heads of the crowd. More likely the foot of the cross was at eye level. Jesus could see and hear those caring ones near Him. Today we need cousin Johns and Aunt Marys at the foot of the cross, hearing Jesus' voice because they're near Him and stretching their arms out to enclose others because they are standing among them!

The Word of Loneliness

Prayer

Almighty God, who hast shown us in the life and teaching of Thy Son the true way of blessedness, Thou hast also shown us in His suffering and death that the path of love may lead to the cross, and the reward of faithfulness may be a crown of thorns.

Give us grace to learn these hard lessons. May we take up our cross and follow Christ in the strength of patience and the constancy of faith; and may we have such fellowship with Him in His sorrow, that we may know the secret of His strength and peace, and see even in our darkest hour of trial and anguish the shining of the eternal light. Amen.

—From an old book of prayers for students

12

THE WORD OF LONELINESS

By Millard Osborne

And at the ninth hour Jesus cried with a loud voice . . . "My
God, my God, why hast thou forsaken me?" Mark 15:34.

He hung suspended from the rough beams of a heavy
cross a few feet off the ground. He suffered the humiliation of death as a criminal. He was buffeted by the jeers
of the bystanders and the passing crowd. It is not possible
for us to realize fully all that Jesus Christ endured in
those hours from midmorning to midafternoon when he
was exposed to the world and the powers of darkness in a
most vulnerable way.

To be the light of the world, the bread of life, the Son
of God, and then to not only be rejected, but also reviled,
spat upon, falsely accused, and crucified—to offer salvation to a perishing world and in return be crowned with
thorns and planted between the thieves—to hang in
darkness, to feel the impact of sin, to look into the face of

Millard Osborne, Harper, Kansas, was a pastor at Lebanon, Oregon. Since
1970 he has served as Conference Minister for the South Central Mennonite
Conference.

death and to feel alone—all this we glimpse in Christ's words from the cross, "My God, my God, why hast thou forsaken me?" (Mark 15:34).

1. Cry of Despair?

Was Christ, as He uttered this fourth statement from the cross, merely discouraged? Was He simply weary, tired, and aching in body and soul? Were these the words of depression? Or disillusionment? Or despair? Had He expected God to intervene? Was He facing temptation even at this moment to recant His faith in God? To violate His pledge of obedience?

He had hung three hours on the cross before noon. Then darkness came. For three more hours in the dense darkness which blocked out the sunshine of midday, the Savior was exposed to the loneliness of humiliation. The demeaning experience which was His in this hour was as dark as midnight in an underground cavern.

We can safely assume that the darkness was not only a fact of the day's appearance, but also an accurate description of Christ's experience. A darkness of body, soul, and spirit. The physical torture of crucifixion, with excruciating pain, sent waves of darkness coursing through the victim's body.

In the dark hours as life draws near its end, it is only natural for one to draw back from death, from the tearing apart of body and soul. But Christ had committed Himself to this hour. Long ago He had set his face to go to Jerusalem. When the Master told His disciples that He must die on the cross, Simon Peter objected. But the Master rebuked Peter and said he did not know the things of God. The cross necessary for Christ to be the Savior of the world. So our Lord took for Himself this place of sorrow and suffering. He gave Himself to this death on the cross.

Although He was killed by the treachery of the Jewish leaders, it was within the will of God, and the will of Jesus Christ Himself. This was His chosen path of obedience to His heavenly Father. Thus the darkness of the cross was no surprise to the Savior.

2. Cry of Suffering?

In the words of this middle saying from the Cross, Christ turned, as far as the cross experience was concerned, from the part of His mission which was earth-focused. Earlier He had reached out with loving words for those who crucified Him, for the thief seeking pardon, and to those loved ones who needed to hear His words of care and concern. Now he addressed His words to His Father in heaven.

"My God, my God, why hast thou forsaken me?" are the words of the Suffering Savior who, at the moment of His supreme self-sacrifice, felt acutely the weight of the burden which was His as He took upon Himself the sin of the whole world. In the dark hours, Christ felt a deep sense of being forsaken by fellow human beings as well as a sense of being forsaken by God. God was silent. Had He really withdrawn from His Son?

G. Campbell Morgan referred to those words from the lips of Christ when he wrote, "It is the cry of One who has reached the final issue of sin. It is the cry of One who has fathomed the deepest depth of sorrow. It is the cry of One Himself o'erwhelmed in the mystery of silence."

God *gave* His Son to be crucified (not just *permitted*). God was in Christ reconciling the world to Himself. Through the cross experience, God satisfied His own claims upon us through Christ. When Christ died, the sacrifice we could not offer was offered for us. The debt we could not pay was paid for us. The good news is that all that is required of us is already accomplished for us in reconciling us to God.

In the National Gallery of Art hangs a unique painting of Calvary. The figure of Christ on the cross is almost hidden in the darkness. At first glance, one sees nothing more than the dim figure of the Suffering Savior. But as one looks more intently, one sees another figure with arms outstretched, tenderly supporting the Suffering One. His face is twisted by pain which is more intense than that of the crucified Christ. The artist intends to show that God, the Father, is grieving and suffering with His Son, as he hangs on the cross.

In the midst of the darkness of the crucifixion, God is love. He is suffering with Christ, for the human race. God demonstrates here the extent of His devotion to us through Jesus Christ. Christ suffered for us in lonely darkness.

3. *The Pain of Loneliness*

In earlier, brighter days the Master had known and experienced joy and happiness. Surrounded by the crowds, His closer circle of loyal followers, and those seeking His loving touch, He had delighted in human companionship. He had even enraged the religious leaders by His association with obvious sinners and his apparent enjoyment of those occasions. There were the children and their parents coming to see Him. There were dinners and many times of fellowship. There were the shared experiences of health restored and broken lives healed. And many more. The Master thoroughly enjoyed His ministry among people.

The Master also knew sorrow and tears. Jesus Christ experienced disappointment, frustration, weariness, bereavement, rejection, and suffering during His earthly ministry. But the pain of loneliness on the cross was deeper than all that had happened before in His earthly life.

The most acute kind of loneliness is not caused by the absence of other persons. It is the aloneness that engulfs us when we are unable to sense that others are sharing, caring, supporting, or identifying with us in a time of great need. To be in the midst of people and not be able to sense that others know, or care to know, what is happening inside you—that is a loneliness which separates and isolates. To be in a circle of friends and not be able to point to one person who is able to understand, or enter into, a difficult experience with you—that is loneliness.

A young father was traveling in a car with two friends. He was facing the uncertainties of his first hospital experience. The diagnosis was serious. Surgery was recommended. The outcome was uncertain. The young man was sure his traveling companions were unaware of his situation. So he began to share with them the experience he was facing. The quick response of both his friends was to launch into accounts of their own first hospital experiences, complete with all the humorous details. The young father who had reached out for understanding and support, now experienced a deeper level of loneliness—and suffered in silence.

Or consider another example. An afternoon call to a pastor brought him that evening to the home of a middle-aged couple. They were stable members of his congregation. They gave willingly of their time, skills, and other resources for the work of the church. Their children were now grown and gone.

As the couple and their pastor visited, they shared the reason they had called him. They felt a growing concern for one of their children. It seemed obvious to them that their child, married and living in another community, was making decisions which were inconsistent with a commitment to Christ. And so the parents talked over their concerns about their child, but also their own growing concern about their effectiveness as parents. Had they failed somewhere in the nurturing years of child bearing? The gnawing fear that they had been inadequate as parents caused them times of soul-searching and regret about real or imagined omissions.

The pastor, not inclined to take people seriously, listened awhile to these dear people in their heartfelt plea for understanding and pastoral care, and then ended the visit shortly with a figurative pat on the back and a brief pep talk. The couple sat silently. Their pain of loneliness deepened.

In the dark hours on the cross our Lord must have felt utterly alone. The bulk of His disciples and followers had fled. The few who stood close by seemed too bewildered to extend support to Him. They were caught up in their own grief and suffering. The crowds jeered. The soldiers had done their work and waited as disinterested spectators. The religious leaders were satisfied that they were finally rid of this troublemaker. Even the two thieves who were sharing a common experience with Him, were unable to identify with our Lord in His self-giving act of obedience, His love-gift to the world.

Oh, the wrenching pain and twisting agony to discover, at a time of greatest need, that no one seems able or willing to extend a caring, supportive touch of love and concern. That is the deepest pain of loneliness. Thus did Christ verbalize His agony when He cried out, "My God, my God, why hast thou forsaken me?"

4. Cry of Victory!

Although these words from the cross are heavy with pain and agony, they do not include the aspects of desperation or dereliction. Instead these words include an element of trust. In Psalm 22 these words introduce a psalm of faith and praise. There David describes the experience of a righteous person living in an evil, hostile world. One does not expect the world to be the source of strength, comfort, and hope. That alone comes from our Creator God. In turning to God in His darkest hour of suffering and loneliness, Christ shows us the way to meet the darkness. As F. W. Krummacher wrote, "By the repetition of the words, 'My God,' He makes it evident that solely by means of His naked faith He had struggled through all opposing feelings; and that God was still His God."

At the brink of death, when the darkness around him and within him threatened to blot out entirely the light of truth and righteousness, Christ held off the threat by turning his attention to His God. These words form a cry for help out of His helplessness, a cry of childlike confidence out of His loneliness.

By His example Christ shows us the way to face the darkness. Though we may be alone without the support of friends, without the necessities of life, without physical strength, and though we may not be strongly aware of God's presence, still He Himself is always near. He is responsive to our needs and reaches out to us with His touch of love.

In the book, *Cry, the Beloved Country*, the story centers around Stephen Kumalo, an aged black pastor in South Africa. Pastor Kumalo's life is filled with the pain and sorrow brought on by racial tensions. He loses a wayward son, who is hanged for his misdeeds. Following all this, Pastor Kumalo was able to say, "I have never thought that a Christian would be free of suffering. . . . For our Lord suffered. And I come to believe that he suffered, not to save us from suffering, but to teach us how to bear suffering. For He knew that there is no life without suffering."

The Word of Human Need

The Hill Called Norbury

I seldom pass
This wind-torn tree,
Or walk this hill,
Or tread this grass,
But I do see
Another tree,
Another hill,
Another grass.

—Egbert Sandford

13

THE WORD OF HUMAN NEED

By Robert Hartzler

Jesus, knowing that all was now finished, said . . . "I thirst."
John 19:28.

As a boy of nine I helped survey our timberland in the mountains of central Pennsylvania. It was rough terrain difficult to walk let alone carry the rods and chains. We left the water in the truck knowing we couldn't carry it on the job. We mistakenly expected to find fresh springs along the way. At noon we ate dry sandwiches and talked about what we would give for a drink of water. By two o'clock I wondered whether I'd make it. All afternoon I thought of cool, clear water. We finally finished the job and returned to the truck, twelve miles of dense brush and eight hours later, dead tired and dreadfully thirsty. The water was more welcome than any food I have ever tasted.

All of us have experienced thirst at the end of a long

Robert Hartzler, Washington, Iowa, has held several pastorates in Iowa, was youth secretary in Iowa and Nebraska, and presently is pastor in Washington, Iowa.

journey. As the cars turns into the drive we just can't wait to get to that pitcher in the refrigerator. No water satisfies like the water from our own well or city system. How good it is to drink long and deep of one's own special water!

Jesus died a Man. Not only a courageous and strong Man full of heart, He was also a sensitive and loving Man full of human hurt. The thirst in his throat was as real as the dryness of the dustiest desert on the face of the earth.

Jesus was thirsty—terribly, excruciatingly, and humanly in need of water. How long had it been since he drank? We don't know. The Roman scourging took its toll of body moisture early in the day the order to crucify was given. The long march to Golgotha bearing the heavy wooden instrument of death certainly dehydrated the body further. There was lightning and thunder early in the afternoon. Perhaps it was one of those warm stormy spring days when all of nature seems to cry out for rain. Suspended between heaven and earth, with nails through hands and feet, the vital juices dripped and evaporated a drop or two at a time. He was dying the slow death of exposure to the elements. Is it any wonder that He cried out, "I thirst"?

1. A Long and Difficult Journey

It had been a long hard journey for the carpenter from Nazareth. Mary had probably told Him about the rude circumstances of His birth in the stable. Away from home in an uncomfortable and unsympathetic setting, His first cry joined the chorus of troubled animals in the stall. And here at the end He cries out again for something wet to cool the ravaging thirst of an abused body.

How old was the lad when He learned about the sudden flight to Egypt? Had Joseph hid the fact of His exile? How old must one be to understand the cruel actions of a king threatened by a babe at his mother's breast? And now Christ continues to threaten with the turned cheek and nonretaliatory attitude.

The growing-up years must have been long and difficult also. Children can be cruel. They don't exactly relish special peers. And Jesus must have been special. His understanding at age twelve tells us something about His own self-concept. I suppose He grew tired of being singled out by His peers as a little bit different. As an adolescent He probably longed to drink the water of average acceptability.

And the three short years of public ministry may have seemed an eternity. Sleepless nights in the wilderness without food or water. No home or retreat except what He could find in nature. And always the constant hypocrisy and carping of His own people. Watch Him offer the woman of Samaria water which would cause her to never thirst again!

2. *The Thirst of Death*

But by far the longest and the thirstiest journey was the way of the cross. Even the Romans didn't have much stomach for a crucifixion. One way to avoid the long wait for death on the cross was to see that the criminal was half dead before you hung him up there. And there were ways.

First came the scourging. Tie him to an X-shaped wooden frame with back bare and bent to prevent movement. Then lay on the lashes—thirty nine of them. Long leather thongs with pieces of bone and metal literally tear the flesh to shreds. Some go insane, some merely faint, and many die before leaving the frame. Then make him carry his cross. Make him carry it through every avenue, street, and alley in town—the longest possible route—that people may learn to properly respect authority.

Jesus was too far gone to carry it very far. As they hung Him up He refused the anesthetic and the thirst raged on. After three hours he said, "I thirst." It was the understatement of the day.

I have sat by dying persons until the death angel arrived. Dry feverish lips often cry out for water. The mind slips back to that favorite drinking place in life. The spring in the pasture, the well in the yard, the tin cup on the fence all take their special place at the end of a long dry journey.

Jesus did not die of thirst, but He died a thirsty man. His thirst was real and pronounced and He chose to express it in the agony of death. How genuine and human the simple statement, "I thirst!"

3. The Mark of Full Humanity and Character

It was the sign of His full humanity. This was no special freak combination of divine flesh oblivious to human appetites and needs. He was in every respect subject to the hurts and exigencies of the human condition. The only difference between Jesus and us was that He didn't deserve it and we do.

This word from the cross dramatizes the character of Jesus. He expressed His thirst only after the needs of others had been met. The thieves to either side had received His forgiveness and pardon. John had agreed to care for Jesus' mother. And then He said, "I thirst."

How true to form! Jesus thought of others first. He had

that rare ability of perfecting personal priorities. God's will came first, followed by other person's needs, and then He was free to consider His own aching body.

There is an acronym which says it well for disciples. J-O-Y stands for Jesus first, others second, and yourself last. The writer to the Hebrews points to Jesus as our example, "who for the joy that was set before him endured the cross."

How many of us have been willing to serve God and others to the point of physical thirst? When we do a neighborly deed we expect at least some food and water in return. Barn raisings and plowing bees for the sick or unfortunate are accompanied by plenty to eat and drink. Even Mennonite Disaster Service efforts are blessed with sandwiches and water. And when such is not the case we grumble silently if not aloud.

Let Jesus' suffering and death instruct us. Only after the needs of others were met was He free to say, "I thirst." Yet it is in the position of a thirsty person that Jesus comes to us today.

Just a few days before His arrest Jesus had spoken about the coming judgment. The King will welcome those who among other things gave Him a drink when He was thirsty. But those who turned a deaf ear to the cries of human need will be banished from the King's presence. And who was the King? Jesus! And how do we serve Him now that He has ascended? By serving the least of our fellowmen!

Do we find it hard to minister to the needs of the least of these? Are our spirits and attitudes open and positive toward the poor? Or, do we rankle and curse at the welfare rolls? Thirst holds no nationality, race, nor ethnic origin. It is a fact of life. We do well to remember that the neighbor without water is a thirsty Jesus. "As you did it to one of the least of these my brethren, you did it to me" (Matthew 25:40).

4. His Thirst Continues

Jesus died a thirsty Man. And His thirst continues right into the twentieth century. He is thirsty in the Sahel of north central Africa where life continues to deteriorate and disappear. Christ is thirsty in India where there is never enough protein to go around. Christ cries out for water in the war-torn regions of Indochina where a so-called Christian country impeded civilization by at least a decade. He thirsts in Harlem and Watts and Chicago's southside, in Appalachia, and in every corner of this earth where dire human need persists.

His cry for water is not limited to water. It is the cry of human need on a thousand different levels in a million different places. It is the need of the prince and the pauper, the sinner and the saint, the powerful and the dispossessed. But most of all it is my need.

5. He Was Thirsty for Me

When Jesus died in the agony of burning thirst He was suffering for me. "Surely he has borne our griefs and carried our sorrows. . . . He was wounded for our transgressions, he was bruised for our iniquities. . . . Because he poured out his soul to death, and was numbered with the transgressors" (Isaiah 53:4, 5, 12).

Isaac Watts has said it so well: "Alas! and did my Savior bleed? And did my Sovereign die? Would he devote that sacred head, for sinners such as I?"

Yes, He would and did. Jesus died a thirsty Man that we might be able to drink of the water of life freely.

6. A Thirsty King

A story from the Old Testament illustrates the compassion and purpose of the suffering Savior. It comes from the life of King David, not from the narrative but from the list of David's mighty men and their deeds in 2 Samuel 23. Three of David's mighty men are unnamed but they will be remembered for their deed.

It was harvesttime in Palestine, the hottest part of the year. David was holed up in the cave of Adullam, for the Philistines were in control of Judea. And as David literally sweated it out in the cave he thought of the cool clear waters of the well in Bethlehem, which is by the gate!"

Subsequently the three unnamed men fought their way through the enemy lines, drew water from the king's favorite well, bringing it safely back to their lord, King David. And what did David do with the water? Did he drink it eagerly or sip each delicious drop? Did he gulp it down to quench the fires of dehydration? Did he swill it noisily letting it run down the chin and beard? No. He didn't drink it at all but rather poured it out on the cave floor as an offering to God, saying, "Far be it from me, O Lord, that I should do this. Shall I drink the blood of the men who went at the risk of their lives?"

When Jesus expired at Calvary, He died in the throes of intense physical thirst. There were no mighty men there to show themselves strong on His behalf. They had all fled and forsaken Him. Only a nameless bystander offered the Lord of glory some vinegar on a sponge. Have you ever tried to drink vinegar from sponge? Try it sometime, and good luck!

The two simple words, "I thirst," are powerful witnesses to the fact of Jesus' full humanity. His thirst identifies Jesus of Nazareth as a Man very much in touch with the human condition.

"Since then we have a great high priest who has passed through the heavens, Jesus, the Son of God, let us hold fast our confession. For we have not a high priest who is unable to sympathize with our weaknesses, but one who in every respect has been tempted as we are, yet without sinning. Let us then with confidence draw near to the throne of grace, that we may receive mercy and find grace to help in time of need" (Hebrews 4:14-16).

The Word of Victory

It Is Finished

People today still marvel at the genius of Michelangelo. His skills in architecture, painting, and sculpture are known the world around. His finished works such as his statues of Moses and David are well known. What many do not know is that, because of his temperamental nature, he left most of his sculpture unfinished. In the new Sacristy of Michelangelo in Florence, Italy, you may visit an entire hall filled with the unfinished works of Michelangelo.

Many scholars and workers down through the centuries have left important parts of their work unfinished. Books and works of art lay incomplete in study and studio. Most had planned to complete their work, but life ended.

Not so with Jesus! He finished the work He had come to do. He is the Author and Finisher of our faith. Nothing more is needed for our salvation.

—John M. Drescher

14

THE WORD OF VICTORY

By Richard A. Showalter

He said, "It is finished"; and he bowed his head and gave up his spirit. John 19:30.

Sir Christopher Wren, the famous English architect, designed a span for the Thames River named the Waterloo Bridge. It was a model of tasteful engineering. But during the war of 1914-18, German bombs were dropped nearby. One pillar of the bridge sank, forcing the British to spend thousands of pounds each year to keep it in repair.

Engineers came from many parts of England to attempt to discover why one pillar sank, but not the other. The answer was found in the bridge itself—faulty construction.

For when the wooden piles forming the foundation of the sinking pillar were examined, it was found that *one* of the piles was a quarter inch shorter than the others. One

Richard A. Showalter, Irwin, Ohio, served as assistant to the president and instructor in biblical studies at Eastern Mennonite College, Harrisonburg, Virginia. From 1972 to 1974 he was a pastor in Indiana. Presently he is on the faculty of Rosedale Bible Institute, Irwin, Ohio.

quarter-inch fault spelled failure when the test came. The bridge had been finished—yet not quite.

Jesus said, "It is finished"—said it in the middle of the blackest day of His life. Heaven and earth alike were closed to His cries. Who could have guessed that *anything* was finished? To the contrary, everything had fallen apart.

But unlike man's achievements marred by unseen but fatal flaws, God's projects, when finished, are truly complete—even though all reality seems to witness against them.

What words those were for a dying man! Consider the alternatives.

1. Defeat and "Immortality"

"I am finished! I'm licked!" Everything in my humanity regards death as the great defeat. When death approaches, *I* am finished. My hopes, my goals, my friends, my life itself—all is somehow conquered in the pervasive and mysterious stalk of death.

Nothing evokes my deepest human passions like death, especially when my own life is at stake. The endless quest for healing, whether in the scientific methodology of modern medicine or in the prayer of faith in the Christian church; the awful aura of an Auschwitz memorial with its ovens, suitcases, and rows of barracks; the daily preoccupation with the threat of meltdown in a nuclear plant, earthquake in a city, starvation on a continent, war in the world—all fascinate and repel the human mind in countless patterns. All because death finishes me. I'm licked.

To solve the problem we seize upon "permanent contributions" or "immortal art" or "enduring institutions" or "good children." Alexander died at thirty-two, but he sculpted the Hellenistic world. Socrates left no writings, but we have his genius through Plato. Susanna Wesley was an unremarkable homemaker, but she blessed the Christian church with a John and Charles. Milton died blind, but he gave the world a *Paradise Lost.* Yes, I too will die, but not before. . . .

Jesus died. Just died. No children, no books, no political conquests, no paintings, no band of faithful disciples (they had scattered). He died in thorough rejection—by a close friend, His own people, the Romans, the world He knew. Yet there is no trace of defeat, no "I'm licked." Just the enigmatic words, "It is finished."

2. Competitive Triumphalism

"He is finished! I won!" Perhaps the keen eye of Jesus pierced the cosmic curtains surrounding nondescript, tiny Judea; perhaps in that moment His mind traced the outlines of a victory unapparent to the motley group about the cross. Perhaps.

However, there is no hint here of the final jibes of an expiring competitor. No "I who am about to die, greet you!" No "Your turn is next!"

For Jesus had no competitors. Christians have sometimes heard His final words in the context of a gigantic struggle with Satan for universal victory—a battle which was nip and tuck to the finish.

But he had already declared, "I saw Satan fall like lightning from heaven" (Luke 10:18). He already held the key to martial triumph; He had His twelve legions and more. He had His victory secured. He did not have to die, for He had no competitors. No, "He is finished" here.

3. Passive Resignation and "Resurrection"

"You are finished!" You've done what you could to make the world a better place. Death comes; further struggle is useless. Bow reverently before the great inevitable, and submit.

All that you have been has now entered the stream of history—your miracles, your exorcisms, your teaching, your love. The cup of hemlock gently taken may for you, like Socrates, yet demonstrate to a watching world the imperturbability of noble character, the freedom of a liberated spirit. Equanimity in the face of death is the last lesson you must model for your disciples. Your spirit has now entered history to be reborn in the lives of all who are influenced by the power of your example, who decide to become new men. Whatever men decide about God, you, at least, cannot be evaded.

You are finished—so what? Your spirit lives on.

But this is no more than a Hegelian caricature of the spirituality, the *definiteness* about God, which Jesus assumed. Whatever His cry meant, it must have meant more than this.

4. The Kingdom Is Here

Defeat, immortality, triumphalism, resignation, resurrection of Spirit—all of this is carelessly and frequently read into the final words of Jesus, even by His disciples. What else could possibly be meant, after all? But there is another answer.

It leaps from page after page of the gospels and resounds through history in the lives of His saints. *The kingdom is here!* Its proclamation and demonstration is sealed for all ages in a life of total obedience to the will of the Father. Where the King rules, there His kingdom has come. So it was that His life is summed up over and again by the words, "I must preach the good news of the kingdom of God" (Luke 4:43) and "the Son can do nothing of his own accord but only what he sees the Father doing; for whatever he does, that the Son does likewise" (John 5:19).

Yet Jesus is acutely conscious that though the kingdom had come in His very person and, therefore, that He can announce it with consummate authority, He nevertheless marks in His person a double transition, not a single. This He does as He who comes and He who sends.

There was a time before He publicly announced the kingdom that He told his mother, "My hour has not yet come" (John 2:4). How His hour did come! It came with power in healing, proclamation, exorcism, love. Its coming marked the transition from the old to the new, the coming of the kingdom in Jesus.

5. *The Era of the Spirit*

But now His hour has come and gone, and He marks another transition with the cry and the whispered groan, "It is finished." In the peace of Gethsemane He had already alerted His disciples to the coming of the second transition when He said, "It is to your advantage that I go away, for if I do not go away, the Counselor will not come to you" (John 16:7).

If the era of tutelage as children under the law (Galatians 4:1-6) passed with the coming of Jesus, and if the era of proclamation and demonstration of the reality of full sonship in the life of one Man passes with the death of the One (John 19:30), then with this utterance we stand at the brink of the era of the Spirit, the presence of the kingdom unbound from the One to the many. Praise

God! The rest of the New Testament is no more, and no less, than the unveiling of that third era. The Holy Spirit is the Spirit of Christ unbound.

6. *What Is Complete?*

Since that cry, and the coming of the new era in completeness, the echoing heart cry of kingdom citizens can be for nothing greater than the full release, in experience, of that unbinding.

D. L. Moody, the nineteenth-century evangelist (and Christian pacifist), said, "I was crying . . . that God would fill me with His Spirit. Well, one day, in the city of New York—oh, what a day!—I cannot describe it, I seldom refer to it—it is almost too sacred an experience to name. Paul had an experience of which he never spoke for fourteen years. I can only say that God revealed Himself to me, and I had such an experience of His love that I had to ask Him to stay His hand. I went preaching again. The sermons were not different. I did not present any new truths; and yet hundreds were converted. I would not now be placed back where I was . . . if you should give me all the world."

Set in this context, the cry from the cross is both an ending and a beginning, a cry of completion that mattered, the surrender of life itself to the Father who orchestrates all.

With this, however, the substantial meaning of "It is finished" is only barely unwrapped. *What* is complete? To unravel the answers more fully would be to undertake an exposition of the nature of the kingdom itself, to explain all the gospels and epistles alike. Yet two observations will underline the distinctiveness of Jesus' words in the face of death.

First, Jesus is simply confessing the conclusion of an obedient life. He knew that "all was now finished" (John 19:28). He understood full well that "the sting of death is sin" (1 Corinthians 15:56), but He faced death without that incompleteness which marks death for every disobedient alien from God, for He had lived in unbroken communion with the Father.

The nagging question in the face of death is always, "What would I have done differently if I could do it over again?"—an implicit confession of sin. But Jesus never asks that question. He only asserts with confidence born of perfect knowledge, "The embodiment of the kingdom in word and life and death, that for which I came—it is finished." It is this embodiment which even in the moment of death became a gift for countless other sons and daughters in the approaching era of the Spirit.

Second, Jesus is sealing an absolute witness to the posture of vulnerability and dependence as the attitude of the kingdom (Philippians 2:5-8). Finished is a life and work of absolute dependence upon the will of the Father; all the Father has is the possession of the Son, including His power. But the Father's power is exercised *for* every one—in release from disease, demon possession, ignorance, and sin. Never has it happened that the Son has directed a miracle *against* a person. Now in the face of violent death there remains the same consistent display of the Father's redemptive love, the refusal to strike back, to win the kingdom's acceptance by force or even by mere display of power. Rather, there is the quiet confidence that completion is real, all appearances to the contrary notwithstanding.

So it remains. It is finished—eternally. Not in defeat, immortality, triumphalism, resignation, or resurrection of Spirit. But in the life and death of one Man for all, embodying the kingdom and releasing its reality for all through the Spirit.

Yet we do well to beware lest that which is victory for Jesus and victory for His brothers and sisters (Hebrews 2:11) is lost to us in experience.

An elderly mountain lady living in a shack was approaching starvation. She received regular mail from a son who had promised to support her when he left home, but the money did not come.

She shared her plight with a neighbor, who asked about her son. "He sends me letters," she said, "and always encloses pretty little pictures, but I never get any money."

"Could I see the pictures your son sends?" asked the neighbor after a time. The poverty-stricken lady took him to her bedroom and showed him the rows of "pictures" tacked on the wall—bank checks worth thousands of dollars!

The victory is complete, the Lord is in His inner sanctuary. Am I banking on what is also mine?

The Word of Commitment

Charles Simeon of Cambridge University in England, conversing with Professor Gurney many years ago said:

Should you see a poor maniac knocking his head against a wall and beating out his brains, you would not be angry with him however he might taunt you. You would pity him from your very soul; you would direct all your energies to save him from destruction!

So it will be with you: the world will mock and trample on you; a man shall come, and, as it were, slap you on the face. You rub your face, and say, "This is strange work. I like it not sir." Never mind, I say, this is your evidence; it turns to you for a testimony. If you were of the world, the world would love its own, but now you are not of the world, therefore the world hateth you.

Many years ago, when I was an object of much contempt and derision in this university, I strolled forth one day, buffeted and afflicted, with my little Testament in my hand. I prayed earnestly to my God that He would comfort me with some cordial from His Word and that on opening the Book I might find some text to sustain me.

The first text which caught my eye was this, "They found a man of Cyrene, Simon by name; him they compelled to bear his cross." You know Simon is the same as Simeon. What a world of instruction was here—what a blessed hint for my encouragement!

To have the cross laid upon me that I might bear it for Jesus—what a privilege! It was enough. Now I could leap and sing for joy as one whom Jesus was honoring with a participation in His sufferings. My dear brother, we must not mind a little suffering. . . . Let us follow Him patiently. . . . We shall soon be partakers of His victory.

15

THE WORD OF COMMITMENT

By David Groh

Then Jesus, crying with a loud voice, said, "Father, into thy hands I commit my spirit!" Luke 23:46.

A man and his young son were walking on treacherous ice. "Give me your hand so that I can hold onto you," the father said. "If you are holding onto me and start to slip, you'll probably let go, and fall." In times of danger we need the reassuring hands of One who is stronger to support and guide us.

1. The Commitment

For six painful hours Jesus had hung upon the cross. Three of those were hours of darkness. What a contrast between the night of His birth and the day of His death! At His birth the creation was overjoyed. An extraordinary star shone. As angels made the announcement, a brilliant glory radiated upon some Judean shepherds in the mid-

---

David Groh, Millersburg, Ohio, has served as pastor and hospital administrator in Puerto Rico and as a pastor in Pennsylvania and Oregon. He is a writer for *Adult Bible Study Guide*, coeditor of *The Ohio Evangel*, and pastor of Millersburg Mennonite Church.

dle of the night. But now the sun became dark, in the middle of the day.

Yet, through the darkness of this hour and the darkness of His own soul, Jesus could see the strong hands of His Father. They would support Him on this final, treacherous journey.

The Old Testament displays the hands of God as powerful. The psalmist pictures Him as the Master Builder, laying the foundations of the earth and sculpting the heavens with His hands (Psalm 102:25). The One who framed the earth continued to control it, from the depths of the earth to the tops of the mountains; from the sea to the dry land (Psalm 95:4, 5). The prophet pictured Him cupping the oceans in His hand (Isaiah 40:12). These powerful hands that created and controlled the earth were also active in the affairs of nations. The right hand of God gave victory (Psalm 48:10).

God not only used His hands for creating and manipulating the big, impersonal world. He also used them for the benefit of faithful individuals. One psalmist saw the hands of God in His own creation. "Thy hands have made and fashioned me" (Psalm 119:73). Another said, "Thou hast given me the shield of thy salvation, and thy right hand supported me, and thy help made me great" (Psalm 18:35).

Into these strong and faithful hands Jesus placed His spirit. "It is a fearful thing to fall into the hands of the living God" (Hebrew 10:31). But Jesus knew of something far worse—to fall out of those hands.

It was His *spirit* that Jesus entrusted to God. At the creation God had taken the first man "and breathed into his nostril the breath of life; and man became a living being" (Genesis 2:7). Now Jesus, as a representative of the new humanity, returned His spirit to its Creator.

As Jesus breathed His last, His life was not being taken away from him. He cried out with a loud voice, not the faint, gasping words of a man whose life was slowly slipping away. In this final act of His will He was making a commitment of the most precious thing that He had, into the hands of the most trusted Person He knew.

The force of the verb indicates that He was entrusting His spirit to God for His personal benefit. For Jesus, the way to greatness was not to grasp for it. Rather, He emptied Himself, became a Servant, and died on the cross (Philippians 2:6-11). He was confident that the one who would receive His spirit would glorify and exalt Him to the place of highest honor.

This final word was addressed to His *Father*. We use a number of words to address our male parent—dad, pop, father, pa, papa, daddy. For Jews of Jesus' day "Abba" was the most intimate and endearing of these terms. This became the normal address of Jesus to God. His fellow Jews would have understood that God was Father of their nation. What was new and startling in His teaching was the way He transformed the idea of God as Father into such an intimate, personal relationship. He lived in complete dependence upon Him.

Jesus taught His disciples what God was like. He was so close that He knew how many hairs they had on their heads. He was so concerned that He saw sparrows fall. He was so loving that He could be compared to the shepherd searching the hills for a stray sheep. He was so forgiving that even the son who had left home and wasted the inheritance was welcomed back with open arms and a great feast. He was so generous that He sent rain not only on the just, but also on His enemies.

This Father forgives even those who do not know the enormity of the evil of their acts.

Because Jesus could pray "Father" in the pain and darkness of this hour, He has the right to expect that His children will address their prayers, "Our Father. . . ."

2. The Lesson

For six painful hours Jesus had hung between life and death. Though death is all about us our society tries to disguise it. The mortician's art attempts to make the dead look alive. Yet, in many of our high schools, where youth are near the peak of physical vitality, the class on death is among the most popular electives.

In His final word Jesus is teaching His followers how to die. He demonstrated that death and life are of one piece. Jesus died as He had lived.

This final word was a *prayer*. For some people prayer is the normal response to any experience. In times of prosperity there is praise. When a need arises there is intercession. At points of crisis there is petition. In failure there is confession. This does not come naturally. It is learned through an attitude of dependence upon God and with much practice.

It is not surprising to hear a prayer as the last word of Jesus. What was more typical of His life? He prayed before He selected the Twelve. Early in His ministry He spent a night in prayer as He determined how far His activity should extend. He prayed at the tomb of His friend Lazarus. The previous night He agonized in the garden seeking the course God would have Him take. Jesus died as He had lived, with a prayer upon His lips.

This prayer was not of His own creation but a quotation of *Scripture*, from deep in His heart. He adapted it to this special need. As He had done so often, Jesus reached back into the Psalms. A Hebrew saint was in distress. Emotionally He was in grief. Physically his body was deteriorating. Socially He was slandered. Politically he was being undermined. He cried for help. He trusted the hand of God to rescue him (Psalm 31:5).

Now Jesus was in a situation similar to that ancient saint. Out of the reservoir of Scripture within Him this prayer gushed forth, but with one significant change. It was addressed to "Father."

As with prayer, the appropriate use of Scripture does not come automatically. For us, as for Him, this response comes from the long practice of meditating upon God's Word. For the one who as a boy had sat among the scholars of His Father's house to hear and to question; who had repulsed the tempter with words from the law; who had expounded its meaning to any who would hear, what could have been more natural than to die with Scripture on His lips?

Jesus died *identifying* with the despised of mankind. Two dying criminals hung beside Him. At a little distance from His cross stood some humble souls who had followed Him during His life. How like His life this was! His first visitors were Judean shepherds. He accepted baptism with crowds of admitted transgressors. Throughout His ministry His enemies accused Him of being a friend of prostitutes, drunkards, and other assorted sinners. Some of His closest followers were crude Galileans who were not careful to observe the details of the law. Until the end He was ministering to the needs of sinners. Jesus died as He had lived.

In His death Jesus demonstrates what it means to die. It is not an experience separate from life. Since we can expect to die the way we live, we must live the way we would wish to die. If we would die with the serenity and assurance that the Father will receive our spirits, our lives must be lived in self-giving love, as His was.

3. *The Witness*

For six painful hours Jesus had hung suspended above a cross section of the human race. Some observed His plight with glee; others were unmoved; His closest followers were stunned into silence. But the commitment with which He died had a profound affect upon those who saw it.

The crowds of curious onlookers were moved by this death. Most of them had not been involved in calling for His crucifixion. They simply stopped to see a spectacle on the way to or from the Holy City. But the manner of this death had a profound affect. They wandered off in little groups "beating their breasts." They experienced agony of remorse in what they saw. They accepted personally the guilt of the evil actions of their leaders. These, no doubt, were among the first of the many Jews who joined the church in the days following Pentecost. Witnessing His death transformed their total outlook on life.

The *Roman centurion* in command of the crucifixion made the greatest confession. He had been in the presence of Jesus since the middle of the previous night. He led his band of soldiers to capture a dangerous criminal, but the Criminal gave Himself up without even an attempt to flee.

In the grueling hours of trial, as false charges were hurled at Him, the Prisoner made no counterthrusts. As the Convict was scourged and mocked there was no retaliation. As He was stretched out upon the cross there were no cursing, but only gracious words of forgiveness. For six hours the centurion had observed the dying Prisoner. The witness of this Man struck a cord within Him. "Certainly he was innocent," he said. Mark records his personal confession, "Truly this man was the Son of God!" (Mark 15:39).

The emphasis is on the quality of the person he had observed. "Here is one with characteristics that go beyond humanity. He has qualities that are godlike." The commitment of Jesus in His death witnessed to those who observed it.

Because Jesus had lived the way He was to die, He was able to die the way He had lived—in complete commitment to His Father. He is the supreme example to His followers of how we should live and how we should die. Not many years later, the first of many who would die for their faith in Him had similar words on his lips. As a mob of outraged Jews rushed at him with stones, Stephen prayed, "Lord Jesus, receive my spirit" (Acts 7:59). These have been the words of many faithful since.

In December 1526 a native of Zurich, Switzerland, was arrested and imprisoned. A month later he was sentenced to death because "he wanted to gather those who wanted to accept Christ and follow him, and unite himself with them through baptism."

On January 5, 1527, at three o'clock in the afternoon Felix Manz was taken through the streets of Zurich to the Limmat River. "As a preacher at his side spoke sympathetically to him encouraging him to be converted he hardly heard him; but when he perceived his mother's voice on the opposite bank, together with his brothers, admonishing him to be steadfast, he sang with a loud

voice while he was being bound, '*In manus tuas,
Domine, commendo spiritum meum,*' and the waves
closed in over his head" (*Mennonite Encyclopedia,* Vol.
III, pp. 473, 474).

Jesus' word of commitment in death was also His commitment in life. This word becomes the word of His
faithful followers in both life and death.

Christ's Cross and Ours

John Ruskin wrote, "The Christian church has turned the cross from a gallows into a raft. Christ did not say, 'If any man shall come after me—he shall have smooth sailing.' "

None of us likes crosses; we do almost anything to avoid them. But they are as much a part of life as taxes and breathing and sickness and good health.

Dean Ralph Inge wrote years ago, "I once took a small boy into a cathedral. We entered by the west door, and as our eyes grew accustomed to the dim light, he looked up above the roof screen and said, 'There is a cross up there.' I pointed to the floor and said, 'There is a cross down there.' The whole cathedral was a cross, of course! It was a cruciform building. Chancel and nave for the upright; transept and transept for the crossbeam. It was all cross.

"You can take me to Golgotha and say, 'There is a cross up there.' I point you to the earth and say, 'There is a cross down there.' The cross is inherent in life. It is life's foundation."

So it is that when we learn to appropriate the work of the cross we move on to have wrought in us the way of the cross. The old man in Adam experiences the work of the cross. The new man in Christ is called to embrace the way of the cross.

—John M. Drescher

16
CHRIST'S CROSS AND OURS

By Jacob J. Enz

Then Jesus told his disciples, "If any man would come after me, let him deny himself and take up his cross and follow me." Matthew 16:24.

At Caesarea Philippi. The Lord's own World Conqueror pauses at Caesarea Philippi the place that is named after two great world conquerors in antiquity—Julius Caesar and Philip of Macedon, father of Alexander the Great.

Our World Conqueror is getting His victory parade ready as He starts to move from Caesarea Philippi to Jerusalem. The climax of that great victory parade came during the last week of Jesus' life.

On Sunday they wildly acclaimed Him!

On Monday they plotted against Him!

On Tuesday they maneuvered to trap Him!

On Wednesday one of His disciples sold Him!

Jacob J. Enz, Elkhart, Indiana, served as pastor in Indiana, German professor, magazine editor, and is presently professor of Old Testament and Hebrew at Mennonite Biblical Seminary, Elkhart, Indiana.

On Thursday evening His circle of disciples argued which would have the chief position!

On Friday all His friends forsook Him, one denied Him, another betrayed Him! His enemies murdered Him!

On that black Friday, God pulled the shades on the sun and we call it Good Friday!

The whole catalog of evil was thrown into God's face during that week, and we call it Holy Week!

By what strange arithmetic does God add
Palm Sunday's hypocritical cry,
A beastly betrayal,
An outspoken denial,
A wholesale desertion,
A gross miscarriage of justice,
And a brutal murder of an innocent Man—
Draw a line, add them up, and get a resurrection?

1. The Cross Factor

The mysterious factor in this arithmetic is the cross. We have a good deal of trouble getting the right answers to life because we leave out the cross factor. The disciples of Jesus had the same trouble long before us.

Examination time had come for the disciples. First semester exams were being administered. The place, Caesarea Philippi.

Matthew divides his Gospel roughly into two parts. Both start with the same words, "From that time Jesus began to. . . ." In Matthew 4:17 one reads, "From that time Jesus began to preach. . . ." Matthew 16:21 has, "From that time Jesus began to show. . . ." And with that, the second semester of the disciples' training by Jesus has begun.

But let us look at the questions on the first-semester exam. There are two parts to this test. The first question is, "Who do men say that the Son of man is?" The second, "Who do you say that I am?"

Consider the first question, "Who do men say that the Son of man is?" Throughout the first half of the Gospels his associates have seen His mighty deeds. They have heard His mighty teaching. They have considered His mighty challenge to follow Him. Now He asks His disciples, "Who do men say that I am?"

The answers of the disciples seem to come fast. "Some say John the Baptist, others say Elijah, and others Jeremiah or one of the prophets." Now it may be true that the understanding of the people was not too clear. They did, however, recognize Jesus as a mighty prophet. They observed that He like John the Baptist, Elijah, and Jeremiah was One who ran into real trouble with the people in high positions of authority—both religious and political.

2. Make Up Our Minds—and Our Lives

But on with the examination! The second question was, "Who do you say that I am?" Jesus never leaves us off with discussing Him. He wants us to make up our minds! In the summons of the gospel making up our minds means making up our lives, to use an expression of the late H. E. Fosdick. We shall never understand Jesus as long as we just talk about Him. A part of the gospel epistemology, a part of the gospel way of knowing, is doing. We are so slow to understand that there comes a point where we do not understand more until we have faithfully obeyed and faithfully lived out that which we clearly understand.

Peter, who usually spoke out for the rest, is quick to answer, "You are the Christ, the Son of the living God!"

Most of us would say, "Of course he would say that." Peter had seen His great miracles and heard His dynamic and powerful teaching and preaching.

But there is something here not quite on the surface, at least to those of us who do not know the geography of Palestine too well.

Jesus administers this examination at Caesarea Philippi, at the outermost reaches of his homeland. What is He doing here? Here there were only small groups of Jews. Furthermore, most of his ministry had been in Galilee, a far cry from the seat of authority in Jerusalem where any Messiah should operate. This was no place to gather an army and drive out the hated Romans.

3. *He Threw Away a Throne*

As if that were not enough, He had just sent away the 5,000 He had fed who in their amazement at this miracle had wanted to make Him king! To His disciples He threw away a crown *and* a throne *and* political liberty for His people in this one unthinkable act. Is it any wonder that Judas chose to betray Him thinking that in the last ditch Jesus would call down angels from heaven to carry on His warfare against the Romans? In spite of all this Peter still insists and confesses, "You are the Christ, the Son of the living God." And Jesus is thrilled! "You are Peter, and on this rock I will build my church."

In the Gospel of John a similar incident is told a bit differently. People were leaving Jesus after the hard teaching about eating His flesh and drinking His blood—probably John's way of saying, "Take up your cross and follow me." When Jesus asked His disciples, "Will you also go away?" Peter said, "Lord, to whom shall we go? You have the words of eternal life" (John 6:68). Peter and the disciples were confessing Christ. They were saying, "You are the Christ," in the face of almost insurmountable odds.

Perhaps you may be confessing Christ in the face of insurmountable odds. You joined the ranks of the followers of Christ at a time when life was bright and hopeful for you. Now, suddenly, dark clouds come across the sky of your life—sickness, troubled family relationships, financial problems, bereavement, and perhaps a combination of some of these. You are asking yourself, "Is God still in control of my life? Does He still really care for me?" And out of the agony of your situation you cry with Peter, "You are the Christ" in spite of the fact that life seems to say the opposite is true.

For the disciples, the first semester has come to a close. They have passed the exam and are ready for more advanced work.

The first semester began with the words, "From that time Jesus began to preach. . . ." The second semester begins in Matthew 16:21 with the words, "From that time Jesus began to show. . . ." And what is He showing them? He must go to Jerusalem, not to take His throne as king in the palace, but to suffer many things at the hands of the elders, the chief priests, and the scribes—to be killed and to be raised again the third day.

4. *Words Must Become Deeds*

There comes a time when words must become deeds and acts. Talking sermons must become walking sermons. Testimony of mouth, hand, eye, ear, feet, billfold, bank account—all these are involved in the walking ser-

mons we preach as we follow Jesus in translating His
words into deeds.

To the disciples this did not sound right at all. Go to
Jerusalem? Yes! To suffer and be killed? Unthinkable!
What was worse, the Bible tells us that Jesus was saying
this, not secretly, but openly!

Now Peter goes to work on Him! "Let's be reasonable
about this, Lord!" Jesus answers with a most stunning re-
buke. Peter, whom a few sentences earlier Jesus called
the rock on which He would build His imperishable
church, He now calls Satan.

As if that were not enough, Jesus invites the disciples
to take their cross and come along. They had been in
demonstration school for some two years. Those days are
now over. This is participation school. This is it! Any
other way would have been a complete reversal of the
path Jesus had set for Himself. The shadow of the cross is
over the whole of Jesus' life in all of the Gospels. From
half to two thirds of the Gospels are devoted to the time
between Jesus' first announcement that He would die
and the end. Step by deliberate step He has come to the
moment of this announcement. He submitted to baptism
by John, the man who had made such a scathing denuni-
cation of the religious leaders—probably including
seminary teachers. When John was arrested for being too
specific in his preaching to Herod about his immoral life,
Jesus went out preaching, saying exactly what John the
Baptist had said, "The kingdom has come! Repent!"
They were both in the unpopular business of peeling off
the traditions of men to give justice again. Somehow the
very laws intended to help the poor, the outcasts, and the
downtrodden were used to make them more miserable.
John's fate proved to be Jesus' fate too! The Man who is

to reign finally over the hearts of men must do it from the cross. There is no ultimate power apart from ultimate suffering!

5. *Accomplishment from Defeat*

President Lincoln learned the meaning of building a lifetime of accomplishment out of defeat. He is a superb secular example of suffering as the path of true progress. James Keller, a Roman Catholic, writes, "You can learn from Lincoln that failure isn't fatal." Keller goes on to say (*This Week*, Sunday newsmagazine, February 19, 1957) that "too often it seems to me people lose their courage in facing life because of past failures or fear they may fail in the future. One good way to cure such fears is to remember the story of a man who actually built a lifetime of accomplishments out of defeats. The . . . litany of failures that punctuated his life throughout 30 years is a living and eloquent example of the successful use of defeat in achieving victory." Abraham Lincoln's record is as follows:

1. Lost job 1832.
2. Defeated for legislature 1832.
3. Failed in business 1833.
4. Elected to legislature 1834.
5. Sweetheart died 1835.
6. Had nervous breakdown 1836.
7. Defeated for Speaker 1838.
8. Defeated for nomination for Congress 1843.
9. Elected to Congress 1846.
10. Lost renomination 1848.
11. Rejected for Land Officer 1849.
12. Defeated for Senate 1854.
13. Defeated for nomination for vice-president 1856.
14. Again defeated for Senate 1858.
15. Elected president 1860.

In our reading of the Gospels we have forgotten that what Jesus taught us led directly to what He did for us. Too often we eagerly grasp for the gracious gift of salvation wrought for us through the shed blood on the cross. But we forget that with His blood that saved us He was underscoring and underwriting all of His teaching, including that which asks us to take our cross and follow.

A cross for us? Surely! Crosses are nice in church on our lapels or on a necklace. But Jesus is talking about a cross set up right in the middle of your life and mine. Too long have men and women who claim to be Christian left the cross behind them in church until the following Sunday. D. L. Moody said, "I believe that if there is one thing that pierces the Master's heart with unutterable grief, it is not the world's iniquity, but the church's indifference."

6. At the End of a Countdown

We are surely living at the end of a countdown for the judgment of God on a culture that has pushed the cross out the edge of its life. Personal security, comfortable and well-amused living is at the center. All this is taking place at a time when the world's refugee peoples are growing by the hundreds of thousands! Our comfort so often has been at the price of indifference to the desperate needs of others close at hand or far away.

We are coming to the end of the countdown. Turmoil is breaking forth. Fires are breaking out. Jesus is in the midst of those fires calling us to do the only thing that makes sense at this point in history—take up our cross and follow Him. Are we willing to face what this means for us? An editorial in the *Elkhart Truth* recently pointed out that a knowledgeable person had said what is needed is a massive escalation of war and a declaration of national emergency at home—rugged austerity. Must we wait until the government forces this on us? Is not voluntary poverty the way the cross has always held before us? Are we willing to identify ourselves as did Jesus with the deepest needs of man who is at enmity with himself, his neighbor, and his God and help him up?

We must reckon with the fact that it may not be business as usual in our country. The only security in that situation is faithfulness in the midst of massive disruption. We shall learn what it means to bear the cross. We shall be tempted to think that suffering service and sacrifical giving will hurt us, will set us back. But they are the path of true progress.

Jesus had set His face toward the cross unflinchingly; He invited His disciples to go with Him. The next experience was the transfiguration when the Voice from heaven broke forth in one of the only two times in the Gospels when God Himself spoke. (The first was at the baptism of Jesus.) The Voice said in the hearing of the disciples, "This is my beloved Son; listen to him!" God in heaven and Jesus on earth have prescribed suffering service. Do we dare to walk out on both of them and enjoy our comfortable lives, our highly amused lives while the earth is burning around us?

"O Caesarea Philippi: to accept condemnation of the Way as its fulfillment." So wrote Dag Hammarskjöld. Caesarea Philippi! Two words out of the geography of Palestine from the time of Jesus marked an important fork in the road for Hammarskjöld as noted in *Markings*. Caesarea Philippi, reminder that the gospel at its center has two inseparable crosses, Christ's and yours.

The Rent Veil

James S. Steward, Edinburgh's eloquent preacher wrote:

It is an awful thing to hear Christians, as I heard them, bemoaning the world as pessimistically as any unbeliever. It is a mortifying thing to meet Christians so obsessed with disillusioning problems that they forget the victory of their Master. Do let us believe our own faith. . . . The basic fact of history is not the iron curtain, but the rent veil; not the devil's strategy, but the divine sovereignty. Sursum corda—lift up your hearts!

17

THE RENT VEIL

By Howard H. Charles

*And the curtain of the temple was torn in two, from top to
bottom. Mark 15:38.*

The American poet, Robert Frost, forthrightly expressed his dislike of walls:

> Something there is that doesn't like a wall,
> That wants it down.

He was referring to a stone wall between his property
and his neighbor's. Whether that wall continued to be
mended each spring, or as a result of the poem eventually was torn down, I do not know. That wall, however,
is typical of many other walls both tangible and intangi-
ble, visible and invisible, contemporary and ancient.

Our text speaks of a wall long ago and far away. It was
part of a system of walls, a wall within walls, in the

Howard H. Charles, Goshen, Indiana, has served as a pastor and on numerous denominational committees and boards. He has had teaching ministries in Japan and Ghana and since 1947 has taught at Goshen College and
Goshen Biblical Seminary. Presently he is professor of New Testament at
Associated Mennonite Biblical Seminaries, Elkhart, Indiana.

walled city of old Jerusalem. The reference, of course, is to the veil in the Jewish temple. Let us recall the situation.

The temple area was composed of a central shrine with a series of four surrounding courts. Each court was separated from the other by a more or less well-defined barrier. Beginning from the outermost and moving inward, there were the courts of the Gentiles, the women, Israel, and the priests. Each was more restricted in access. Gentiles could not proceed beyond the first court, women the second, and the lay male Israelite the third.

The central shrine itself had still other segregating barriers. The entrance to the holy place was marked by a large gold-covered door before which hung a richly embroidered veil. In this part of the sanctuary particular priests daily selected by lot discharged their ministry. Beyond the holy place was the innermost room of the sanctuary known as the most holy place. This was separated from the holy place by a double veil embroidered in colors. No one except the high priest was allowed to go behind this veil and that only one day during the year, the day of atonement.

The text speaks of a strange incident that suddenly altered this physical arrangement in the temple. It occurred on the first Good Friday when a Galilean Jew expired on the cross outside the city walls. That day the veil which separated the holy place from the most holy was rent by an invisible hand from top to bottom. No longer was the mystery that belonged to that innermost shrine securely guarded by an unbroken barrier. The wall had been breached.

Let us put this occurrence into its proper context. Who was the one at whose death this unusual event had happened? It was none other than Jesus about whom the whole of the Gospel of Mark speaks. It was He at whose baptism the heavens were rent, upon whom the Spirit descended and who was declared to be God's Son. In the days that followed He crisscrossed Galilee in a mighty ministry of word and deed proclaiming the advent of the kingdom of God. Then one day He left His native province for Jerusalem to press home His message at the very heart of Judaism.

But His call to penitence and faith went unheeded. What was more, His very presence could not be tolerated by His countrymen. Hands were laid on Him. He was nailed to a cross. Suspended between earth and heaven He died. When He breathed His last, the inner veil of the temple, whose outer court He had sought to cleanse, was rent from top to bottom.

No particular significance is attached to this detail either in Mark or the other Gospels. But when it is seen in the larger context of New Testament thought it may well portray some spiritual meaning. What then shall we say about it?

1. Judgment and Forthcoming Destruction

The text may be read as a word of judgment against the temple. It points to its forthcoming destruction. In AD 30 no more than the veil was rent. Forty years later the entire building would be leveled. What was once the pride and joy of Judaism would then be only a memory.

How shall this turn of events be explained? Was not the temple God's gift to His people? Would He then lift His hand against it?

Jesus, according to Matthew, saw an intimate connection between rejection by His people and the future destruction of their temple. This is indicated by the way in which the prophecy against the temple (Matthew 24) is prefaced by the note of negative response in the immediately preceding paragraph (Matthew 23:27-39). Because they would not respond as chicks to a mother hen, judgment would surely follow. "Behold," said Jesus in the temple court, "your house is forsaken and desolate."

The temple was meant to symbolize and to nurture a meaningful relationship between God and His people. But human perversity turned the sign into a guarantee. That which was meant to provide an effective way to deal with human sin often helped to entrench it. The entire order of which the temple was a part was unable to meet the human problem in its deepest form. Unable to achieve God's goal it was destined to be removed.

The rent veil of the temple is a mute reminder that God's hand today just as surely as in the past is against that which will not serve His purpose. Institutions and structures even within the church that are not useful for His ends have the mark of death upon them. Systems of thought and patterns of piety that have become ends in themselves instead of servants of God's Spirit have no meaningful future. Personal interests, activities, and hopes that stand out of relationship to what God is about in our world must sooner or later suffer His judgment. For this reason we may well take to heart David Livingstone's decision as a young man of twenty-one: "I will place no value on anything except in relationship to the kingdom of God."

2. Grace and the New Era

The rent veil speaks not only of judgment but also of grace. It points to the beginning of a new era in God's dealings with us. How shall we speak of the newness which lies embedded in the good news of the gospel?

For one thing, the rent veil may be regarded as an invitation to look anew on the mystery enshrined in the holy of holies. That which was hitherto obscure to the common eye of men now stands exposed for fresh contemplation. And what is it that we see when we gaze into the face of God as seen in Jesus? It is the revelation of love, amazing love, a heart overflowing with love that yearns passionately for our love. This is the uniform witness of the New Testament regarding the meaning of Jesus and His cross. No wonder James Denney after pondering its pages said, "I would like to go into every church in the land and, holding up the crucifix, cry to the congregation, 'God loves like that!' "

But to speak of the rent veil as a window through which we may look with wonder into the heart of God is not all that must be said. It is also a doorway through which the God of the sanctuary strode forth to get under the burden of the world's sin.

Century after century the high priest of Israel on the day of atonement ventured behind the veil to meet God with the blood of a slain animal. But that offering, as the author of Hebrews so eloquently argued, could not deal effectively with the sin problem (Hebrews 10:1-18). Sin is not essentially a stain on the record; it is a disease of the human spirit. To remedy the ill required a fresh act of God that would renew life at its core. God did "what the law, weakened by the flesh, could not do: sending his own Son in the likeness of sinful flesh and for sin, he condemned sin in the flesh . . ." (Romans 8:3). But we should not imagine that God was in safe retreat in the inner sanctuary when Jesus died on the cross. "God was in

Christ reconciling the world to himself" (2 Corinthians
5:19). He was there taking human sin, our sin, to His
own heart and giving back forgiving love.

This great truth is represented in a painting in the National Art Gallery in London. It is a picture of the crucifixion. At first one notices only the figure of Jesus on the
cross. But on closer examination the dim outlines of
another head behind His head, other arms behind His
arms, other feet behind His feet begin to emerge out of
the dark background. Because God was there we may see
in our text a word of grace.

3. *A Privilege for All*

The rent veil symbolizes not only judgment and grace.
It speaks also of our present privilege as Christians. As already indicated, under the old order the right of access
into the throne room of the sanctuary was severely
restricted. Of all the Israelites only one was allowed to
enter. Of all the days of the year only one was marked
with this privilege. Now the situation is otherwise. The
privilege of one person is the opportunity of all. The
blessing of one day is the potential boon of every day.

This great gift of the new order is spoken of in various
passages in Hebrews. Listen, for example, to this one:

> Therefore, brethren, since we have confidence to enter
> the sanctuary [the holy of holies] by the blood of Jesus, by
> the new and living way which he opened for us through the
> curtain [veil], that is, through his flesh . . . let us draw near
> with a true heart in full assurance of faith (10:19-22).

Elsewhere we are invited "with confidence [to] draw
near to the throne of grace, that we may receive mercy
and find grace to help in time of need" (Heb. 4:16). The

throne to which we come is one of grace because we now see the One who sits upon it through the veil rent by the Christ-event. And what we see is a compassionate heart.

Further, we are urged to come "with confidence." We need have no fear or hesitation to speak of anything that is of concern to us. It matters not how great or how small the problems may be that today are troubling us. We may bring them without embarrassment to the God of all grace. And what is more, there is the promise that help is available to us in our need. Let us today in glad faith reach out and lay hold of the proffered aid.

4. A Promise of Perpetual Fellowship

Great as the privileges are which we enjoy today we are still outside the inner sanctuary. The veil has been rent but it has not been removed. But having experienced so much are we not encouraged to hope for yet more? The clearer vision of God that we now have will one day give way to full vision. The freedom of access that is now ours will one day be transmuted into perfect and perpetual fellowship when we shall dwell in the full light of His presence.

The imagery of the temple with its high priest and the day of atonement ceremony which provides the dominant framework of the Book of Hebrews does not readily lend itself to the portrayal of this hope. It is, however, picked up and given powerful expression in Revelation. In the closing chapters of that book we are given to see the new Jerusalem that will descend from heaven in the end-time. In this city there is no temple as there was in Ezekiel's vision of the new Jerusalem many centuries earlier (Ezekiel 40—48). Instead the city itself is described as a perfect cube (Revelation 21:16).

This cubic form is reminiscent of the structure of the holy of holies. But now God's people no longer dwell in some more or less remote court. They are in His immediate presence with the privilege of beholding the full glory of His face. This is the goal toward which the God of the rent veil is moving in His purposes for us. It is not yet a reality. But of its coming there is no doubt in our hearts. For He who is the light of that city is already the light of our lives today.

This then is something of the meaning of our text. It speaks of judgment, grace, privilege, and hope. Surely no one on that first Good Friday could foresee all that would eventually issue through the veil that was then rent. Thank God, today we can say with deeper feeling and more profound meaning than Frost poured into his lines:

> Something there is that doesn't love a wall,
> That wants it down.

This can be our utterance only because it first expresses what was long ago in the heart of God. He, too, didn't love a wall and took steps to remove it. This is why we bless God now and look forward in hope to the day when the last vestiges of the wall will be fully and forever removed.

Risen Indeed!

Lesslie Newbigin *tells the story of a Russian communist leader named Bukharin who in the 1920s went from Moscow to Kiev to address a vast anti-God rally. He ridiculed the Christian faith till there seemed not a stone left in the edifice. At the end of his address there was silence.*

Then questions were invited from the audience. A priest from the Russian Orthodox Church asked if he might speak. When permission was granted, he stood beside Bukharin. Facing the people, he gave them the ancient liturgical Easter greeting, "Christ is risen." Instantly the whole vast assembly rose to its feet as the reply came back like a crash of breakers against the cliff, "He is risen indeed!"

The Communist leader made no reply. There is no reply to faith like that.   —John M. Drescher

Wherever the church has allowed the truth of Christ's victory to get hold of her she has become invincible and irresistible. Her martyrs have sung at the stake and shouted joyous defiance in the teeth of wild beasts in the arena. Whenever Christians believe that Christ is actually risen, immediately the murmuring and whimpering go out of their testimony and the note of plaintive sentimentality goes out of their hymns. Their pronouncements lose the timid tones and become robust and healthy. They go off the defensive and over to the attack. Spring breaks over the churches and fills them with sunlight and fragrance. Such renewals we call revival, and a better name could hardly be found for them, for the word revive means "to live again."   —A. W. Tozer

18

RISEN INDEED!

By David W. Mann

The Lord has risen indeed, and has appeared to Simon!
Luke 24:34.

C. S. Lewis in his spiritual autobiography, *Surprised by Joy* (Harcourt Brace Jovanovich, 1966), tells of his search for joy, a pilgrimage that took him from the childish Christian faith of his early years, into atheism, and finally back to a joyful surrender to the living, personal Lord.

Through the studies and experiences of his school years, Lewis gradually discarded his Christian faith. He was convinced there was no such thing as a personal God and no need for external moral or ethical direction. Nevertheless, the joy he sought to capture seemed to escape him except for occasional, fleeting moments. Above all he detested any external interference in his life, whether by someone who interrupted his thoughts and

David W. Mann, a pastor in Phoenix, Arizona, has served in relief work in Belgium and as pastor in Missouri and Oregon.

study, or by a God who might make demands upon his life.

He describes the journey to faith as a series of moves, as in a chess game, in which God was gently using books and the lives and comments of friends to penetrate the self-sufficient and unbelieving shell he had built around himself. One day, as he was riding on the upper deck of a bus up Headington Hill, he saw himself as being all buckled up in a suit of armor. Before him was a totally free option to either unbuckle the armor or keep it on. He did not feel forced or pressured, but was clearly free to choose either option. He chose to unbuckle.

In that act of surrender he felt as if he were a snowman at long last beginning to melt. At first his belief was only that there is a real and personal God; but when he came to believe that Jesus is indeed the risen Son of God, he discovered the transforming presence of God in his life. The joy he so long had sought came not as a feeling, an experience, or a place, but in surrender to a Person—the living Lord Jesus.

How do we today come to affirm the living reality of Jesus and discover the joy of His presence in our lives? In our Easter songs and affirmations we join with the disciples in the joyous shout of faith, "The Lord has risen indeed!" (Luke 24:34). However we may too quickly overlook the struggle out of which such faith and joy is born.

The appearance of the risen Lord to His disciples was an unexpected and nearly unbelievable surprise. Bound by their own inner conflicts they could not grasp the message of the angels, He has risen, he is not here . . . as he told you." Mark mentions that the women "fled from the tomb; for trembling and astonishment had come upon them; and they said nothing to any one, for they were afraid" (Mark 16:8). When the women reported to the apostles their encounter with the angels, Luke reports, "These words seemed to them an idle tale, and they did not believe them" (Luke 24:11).

Perhaps we can better understand the struggle of faith and the surprise of joy if we look at several of the followers of Jesus and how they came to affirm with conviction, "The Lord is risen indeed!"

1. Mary Magdalene: The Struggle of Grief

Mary Magdalene came to the tomb early on the morning of the first day of the week, heavy with grief (John 20:1-18). Finding the tomb open and the body missing she assumed someone had further desecrated the body of Jesus by removing it. After running to tell the disciples, she returned to the garden to mourn. Although Jesus appeared to her there and spoke saying, "Woman, why are you weeping? Whom do you seek?" she was not prepared to recognize Him. Why was she not able to see Him? The answer is to be found in the struggle of grief.

First, she could not see Him because tears were clouding her eyes, both literally and figuratively. Grief is like pain; it captivates our whole attention. It blinds the eyes of our faith. She was so overcome by her feelings of loss, hurt, and anger that her whole world seemed blurred and distorted. It is sometimes hard to see the presence of Jesus when we are going through the "valley of the shadow."

Second, she could not see because she was busy placing blame: "They have taken away my Lord" (v. 13). "If you have carried him away" (v. 15). When problems overwhelm us, one typical reaction is to find someone to blame. If we can't blame a neighbor, a friend, or an enemy, we may blame ourselves or God. "What kind of a God would let this happen to me?" Or, "If only I had. . . ." One example of this is the way the disciples wanted to fix blame for the problem of the man born blind. "Who sinned, this man or his parents, that he was born blind?" (John 9:2). The resolution of sorrow is never found in pointing fingers. The desire to identify a villain is a normal grief reaction, but healing and faith can only come when we stop trying to fix blame.

Third, Mary was looking in the wrong direction. She was looking toward the tomb rather than to Jesus. When Jesus called her name she had to turn around to see Him (v. 16). A certain amount of mourning is normal and necessary, but a sustained and morbid preoccupation with death can become a blinding bondage. How much better to take our eyes off the grave, the problem, or the tragedy and look into the face of Jesus. Mary could not see the risen Jesus because she was being held captive in her grief.

Mary was surprised by joy when Jesus called her name. "Mary!" Have you ever wondered at the tone and inflection with which Jesus spoke her name? It was like a bell had rung or a light was turned on. Suddenly she awoke to the reality of Jesus' presence and love. The sound of her name, a most personal part of herself, opened her eyes, lifted her burden, and awakened her faith. She was no longer alone and unloved. The depression cycle was broken. The risen, living Lord was standing beside her.

The Lord is risen indeed! He knows *your* name and your needs! The release from the captivity of our grief comes when we hear Him call our name and when we discover the joy of knowing He is present, personal, and that He cares. The joy of the resurrection is found in responding when He calls your name.

2. *Cleopas and the Other Disciple: The Struggle of Mistaken Expectations*

Jesus joined the two people on their dreary walk from Jerusalem to Emmaus (Luke 24:13-35). Being heavyhearted, they were recounting again and again the events of the past three days. Suddenly, they were surprised by the presence and questions of an unknown Person walking with them. "What is this conversation which you are holding with each other as you walk?" he asked (Luke 24:17).

Many pieces of the puzzle seemingly would not fit together. Jesus had been betrayed, tried, crucified, and buried with a rapidity that left them stunned and shaken. The report of the empty tomb and the missing body were confusing enough. But when the women said they had seen a vision of angels who said He was alive, their minds could not comprehend that possibility.

Their greatest block to believing in the resurrection, however, was their mistaken hope. "But we had hoped that he was the one to redeem Israel" (v. 21). They had identified the right person, but they had the wrong expectations. Their dream was to see Jesus use His great powers of deed and word to establish a political kingdom, free from the control of Rome and the tyranny of the religious leaders. But, instead of capturing the seat of temporal power, Jesus was crucified by the powers. Their hopes and expectations were mercilessly devastated in one swift blow.

We too, may be disillusioned when God does not seem to fulfill all the schemes we create for our own plans and desires. "If God is alive and real, why doesn't He bring about all the things I think would be good and right?" We may even have created our own childish expectations of what God is like—an angry policeman, a senile grandfather, a busy administrator of the universe, a demanding perfectionist, and so on. The fears or doubts about our image of what God is like may keep us from discovering the God-who-really-is. The misguided expectations we bring may keep us from seeing the risen, living Lord.

As Jesus walked with the two disciples He explained from all the Scriptures the design of God for the Christ to suffer and enter into His glory. They listened and allowed their expectations to be reshaped.

That evening as Jesus joined them at the table, "He took the bread and blessed, and broke it, and gave it to them. And their eyes were opened and they recognized him" (v. 30, 31). Surprised by joy! Then they recognized the beginning of the dawning of faith, "Did not our hearts burn within us while he talked to us on the road, while he opened to us the scriptures?" Once they allowed their expectations to be reshaped according to the purpose of God, then their eyes were able to see the living presence of Jesus with them. The puzzle began to fit together perfectly.

3. *Thomas: The Struggle of Doubt*

Thomas was not present with the other disciples when Jesus first appeared in the upper room (John 20:24-29). Even though the others had seen Jesus with their own eyes, Thomas refused to accept their testimony. "Unless I see in his hands the print of the nails, and place my finger in the mark of the nails, and place my hand in his side, I will not believe" (v. 25). Thomas wanted to be sure beyond any shadow of doubt.

Not all doubters are the same:

1. There are the belligerent, confirmed skeptics who are committed to a cynical skepticism regardless of the evidence. They reject all evidence which is incompatible with the stance they want to take. They pride themselves in their ability to put down the evidence and the people who share it. They do not want to see or believe.

2. There are the perplexed who are unable to comprehend, or at least to make up their minds. They are caught in vacillating waves of uncertainty, afraid to say what they believe for fear of the possibility of being wrong. They are not willing to risk.

3. There are believing unbelievers, like the father of the boy we read of in Mark 9:24 who said, "I believe, help my unbelief!" This kind of person recognizes the weakness of their faith and the questions with which they wrestle, but are ready to say yes with even a mustard seed of faith. They want to believe and are ready to risk. This last type of doubter might also be called an honest doubter. Thomas was an honest doubter.

Thomas refused to say he believed when he really did not. There is a kind of honesty and integrity in that stand. He was not sure he could trust the testimony of his friends. He may have suspected they were reporting a dream, a hallucination, or an overactive imagination. He wanted to know for himself with hard, firsthand evidence. My faith is strengthened because Thomas insisted on being sure.

Thomas was ready to expose himself to the possibility of the evidence. No longer did he absent himself from the disciple-fellowship. He stayed with them in the upper room. If Jesus might appear again, he wanted to be there to see. His doubt was not a game to play, but a search for truth to grasp. He doubted in order to be convinced.

Thomas was not afraid of the consequences of believing. When Jesus appeared, he dropped his demand to touch and made a full affirmation and commitment, "My Lord and my God!" (v. 28). Thomas' exclamation represented a complete surrender and commitment to Jesus as the divine and sovereign authority for his life. It is one of the strongest affirmations of faith in any of the Gospels.

Jesus honored the honest doubting of Thomas. He appeared again among the disciples and presented Himself to Thomas. "Put your finger here, and see my hands; and put out your hand, and place it in my side; do not be faithless, but believing" (v. 27). Thomas was surprised by joy!

"The Lord is risen indeed!" This central affirmation of the Christian faith sometimes comes through the struggle of a person who sincerely wants to believe but is bound by inner conflicts. This was true for the early disciples and it is true today.

Whether it is in unbuckling the armor, setting aside the captivity of grief, allowing our expectations to be reshaped, or searching in honest doubt, the affirmation of the risen Lord becomes meaningful and personal in the committment and surrender of all we are and hope to be to the presence and lordship of the living Christ. The Lord is risen indeed, and has appeared unto me!

The Resurrection and Daily Life

W. Y. Fullerton *visited a village in Northern Italy in which there is a mimic Calvary. He writes:* "*In ascending order up the hillside a series of chapels have been built, each depicting, with life-size terra-cotta figures, one of the scenes of Jesus' passion—Jesus before Pilate, Jesus shouldering the cross, and so on. The climax was reached with the chapel that showed Jesus hanging on the cross and up to this point the path running between the shrines was well worn by the feet of countless pilgrims, come to look upon their Lord's suffering and death.*

"*But now the path became grass-grown and was clearly little used.*" *Dr. Fullerton however followed on, and, reaching the summit of the hill, found there another shrine, the chapel of the resurrection, which few, it was clear, took the trouble to visit. Most of the pilgrims came to pay homage to a Christ who so far as they were concerned was dead.*

If there is no resurrection the cross is the devil's victory and Christ is a tragic victim. Thank God the cross is not the end. Christ arose.

An unknown poet wrote:

> *He died,*
> *And with Him perished all that men hold dear:*
> *Hope lay beside Him in the sepulchre,*
> *Love grew cold and everything beautiful beside*
> *Died when He died.*

> *He arose*
> *And with Him hope rose and life and light.*
> *Men said, "Not Christ, but death died yesternight!*
> *And joy and truth and all things virtuous*
> *Rose when He rose.*"

—John M. Drescher

19

THE RESURRECTION AND DAILY LIFE

By David Ewert

Blessed be the God and Father of our Lord Jesus Christ! By his great mercy we have been born anew to a living hope through the resurrection of Jesus Christ from the dead. 1 Peter 1:3.

Had the story of Jesus ended with the cross, it would have been unmitigated tragedy. And if Easter were not true, we would be, as Paul admitted (1 Corinthians 15:19), of all people most to be pitied.

Chronologically, the earliest written evidence for the resurrection of Jesus comes from Paul. However, he admits (1 Corinthians 15) Peter and James were dependable sources, together with the "five hundred brethren" who could check and control the tradition (1 Corinthians 15:3-8).

The Gospel records, with all their variations, witness to the great event of the resurrection in such a convincing

David Ewert, professor of theology at Mennonite Brethren Biblical Seminary, Fresno, California, was born in Russia and has served in teaching ministries in India, Europe, and South America.

way that only the most incorrigible skeptic could speak of them as fictitious, as did, for example, the atheist Bertrand Russell, who argues that Christian optimism was "built on the ground that fairy-tales are pleasant." It was the unshakable conviction that Christ was alive that made the disciples of Jesus into such powerful witnesses to a living Christ. The Lord's Day, the New Testament, and the Christian church would all be inexplicable without the resurrection.

The story is told of a meeting between the French philosopher Auguste Comte and Thomas Carlyle. Comte said he intended to found a new religion which would sweep away Christianity and everything else. Carlyle's devasting reply ran something like this: "Splendid. All you need to do is to speak as never man spoke, to live as never man lived, to be crucified, rise again the third day, and get the world to believe you are still alive. Then your religion will have some chance of success."

By the resurrection, as C. S. Lewis observed in *Miracles*, Christ "forced open a door that had been locked since the death of the first man. He has met, fought, and beaten the King of Death. Everything is different because He has done so. This is the beginning of the New Creation: a new chapter in cosmic history has opened."

Little wonder, then, that the early Christians were excited about proclaiming the resurrection of Christ. Not only was the resurrection true, but the message of the resurrection was relevant. However, among those who have no doubts about the resurrection event we often find little to convince us that the great truth of the resurrection has any bearing on life, either.

This article concerns itself with the question: Is the

Christian claim true that the resurrection makes a real difference in everyday experiences? Some of the lines of thought developed here were suggested to me by the reading of Michael Green's booklet, *Man Alive*.

1. The Resurrection and Our Guilt

When the apostles were hailed before the Sanhedrin to answer for the disturbance they were causing by preaching Jesus as Lord they answered (among other things): "The God of our fathers raised Jesus whom you killed by hanging him on a tree . . . to give repentance to Israel and forgiveness of sins" (Acts 5:30, 31).

We all know what it means to feel guilty. It may be caused by an exhibition of greed or lust or temper or dishonesty. This feeling of shame and of failure varies with individuals, depending on the norms according to which their conscience functions. Whenever a person acts contrary to any ideal that he has accepted, he feels guilty (although this feeling of guilt can be lessened by overruling the conscience over a period of time).

However, Scripture insists that we are guilty, whether we feel guilty or not. Our dilemma is not so much guilt feelings (for which there may be a psychological explanation) as real guilt: we are all genuinely morally responsible before a Holy God whom we have affronted and disobeyed. Our guilt is the consequence of our sin and it is with this predicament of ours that Jesus Christ dealt at the cross. He died to settle our debts for us.

For Paul and the other apostles the cross was the burning center of the good news which they preached. But how could a crucified Christ atone for sins? For a Jew, a crucified Jesus meant two things: *(1) That He was not the Messiah*, for instead of leading Israel to victory He went down into ignominious defeat. *(2) That Jesus was under God's curse,* for Deuteronomy 21:23 explicitly stated that a hanged man is accursed by God. The fact that Jesus cried out on the cross, "It is finished," might have been the last step in a great drama of deception but for one thing—the resurrection.

The fact that Jesus arose again is the assurance that He did cope with the load of sin and guilt on our behalf; He did win that titanic struggle with the power of evil. Now we know that His sacrifice is sufficient, that our acquittal is assured, that our sins are forgiven, that our guilt has been removed.

Let us turn to the testimony of the apostles to substantiate further what we have just said. When Peter spoke the good news to those gathered in the house of Cornelius, he recalled that the Jews had put our Lord to death and hung Him on a tree (Acts 10:39). But this was not the end. "God raised him on the third day" (10:40). And what did all this mean? "That every one who believes in him receives forgiveness of sins through his name" (10:43). Our guilt is gone.

Paul and Barnabas, preaching at Antioch of Pisidia, give an extended overview of the history of salvation. The climax of the sermon is the resurrection. "This he has fulfilled to us . . . by raising Jesus" (Acts 13:33); "He whom God raised up saw no corruption" [in contrast to David] (13:37). And what is the upshot of this? "Let it be known to you therefore, brethren, that through this man forgiveness of sins is proclaimed to you" (13:38). The resurrection means that there is no more guilt.

Paul wrote, "[He] was put to death for our trespasses and raised for our justification" (Romans 4:25). "And you, who were dead in trespasses . . . God made alive

together with him, having forgiven us all our trespasses"
(Colossians 2:13). The bill of debt was canceled at the
cross and the evidence for this is Christ's triumph over all
evil powers by His resurrection and exaltation (2:15).

Throughout the centuries men have found in the
resurrection the assurance that God has removed their
guilt. As John Bunyan, in *Pilgrim's Progress*, describes it:
"He ran thus till he came to a place somewhat ascending; and upon that place stood a cross, and a little below
in the bottom, a sepulchre. So I saw in my dream, that
just as Christian came up with the cross, his burden
loosed from off his shoulders, and fell from his back; and
began to tumble; and so continued to do, till it came to
the mouth of the sepulchre where it fell in, and I saw it
no more."

The relief and freedom we enjoy in being able to
dissociate ourselves from the dark deeds we have done or
might do arises out of the fact that Christ atoned for our
guilt on the cross. But this deep assurance of forgiveness
is possible only because we are in fellowship with the
Christ who is alive.

2. The Resurrection and Our Loneliness

Loneliness is one of the great maladies of our modern
generation—a generation more closely tied together by
the mass media and other means than any former generation. This feeling of homelessness and estrangement
strikes young and old, married and unmarried, rich and
poor. People join clubs, attend sports events, hurry to
cocktail parties, crowd theaters and concert halls, but to
no avail.

Paul Tournier, in *A Place for You* (Harper and Row)
points out that every individual wants a place in life and

that our day is suffering from a "vagabond complex."
The mobility of modern man may add to this feeling of
alienation, but there are those who spend much of their
time away from home and yet do not suffer from the ma-
laise of loneliness. Others are always at home but find no
place to stand in life.

Malcolm Muggeridge, in *Jesus Rediscovered* (Family
Library), tells of the awful feeling that crept over him
while with the British forces in Algiers when he first
heard the term "displaced persons" used. He thought
then that it was the most devilish term ever invented.

As we turn to the Scriptures, we find in the first pages
of Genesis the poignant story of how man rebelled
against God, and so became an alien. He lost paradise,
his home. He pushed God out of his life, for he wanted to
live independently of God. And the next tragic step in
the drama of the fall of man was the alienation of persons
from one another—Adam from Eve, Cain from Abel. C.
S. Lewis describes hell as the place where people live
astronomical distances from one another, for the same
selfishness that drives men away from one another (and
that brings them to hell) continues its work there (*The
Great Divorce*).

No one, however, has experienced such utter loneliness as did our Lord on the cross, when even His relationship with the heavenly Father was cut off. He cried out
in anguish, "My God, my God, why hast thou forsaken
me?" No other person has ever experienced loneliness at
such a depth.

But what does this knowledge that Jesus of Nazareth
was the loneliest person who ever lived mean to me? It
means that we will never be abandoned and left to
ourselves, for this same Jesus rose from the dead; He is

alive. The parting words of the risen Christ to His disciples were "I am with you always, to the close of the age" (Matthew 28:20).

But how, we ask, can the risen and ascended Lord be present with us, to overcome our loneliness? Yes, by His Spirit. In His farewell discourses, our Lord promised: "I will pray the Father, and he will give you another Counselor, to be with you for ever, even the Spirit of truth. . . . I will not leave you desolate; I will come to you" (John 14:16, 18). Paul says that in baptism believers are united with Christ in His death and resurrection. We share the resurrection life of Christ through the Spirit (Romans 6:3-5). What transformed the anguish of the Last Supper into the joy of communion the world over was the deep assurance that the Lord was present in the same way in the elements (1 Corinthians 11:26). The short eucharistic prayer (1 Corinthians 16:22 and Didache 10), *"Maranatha,"* means, "Our Lord, come." It was a prayer for Christ to be present at the end of the age. And they knew He was present, for He had promised that where two or three would gather in His name, He would be present. The resurrection opened up the glorious truth of the universal presence of Christ. This presence is very personal, for by His Spirit the risen Lord dwells in every heart. "The Lord is the Spirit" (2 Corinthians 3:17). The risen Lord, who has promised never to leave us or to desert us (Hebrew 13:5), is present in the life of the individual and in the life of the Christian community by His Spirit.

3. The Resurrection and Futility

A frantic search is underway in our day for some cause to live for, something to invest one's life in, some new

frontier to discover. Underneath it all is the haunting fear
that if one hitches the wagon of one's life to a star, that
this star may in the end fall to the ground (as the writer
of the Apocalypse has it). This creeping pessimism seems
to be much more apparent in affluent countries than in
those areas where men still struggle for their livelihood.
A British novelist who had attended the dedication
service of a Christian girl about to leave for the mission
field wrote later that evening in her diary: "Oh, to have
something to live for, entirely, and for ever."

The reason for much of the apathy in the lives of
people today is to be found in the fear that nothing we
give ourselves to will last. Either a world holocaust or
Death, that grim reaper, will destroy our life work. And
Paul was perfectly right when he wrote: "If Christ has
not been raised, our preaching is in vain and your faith is
in vain. . . . Your faith is futile. . . . If for this life only we
have hoped in Christ, we are of all men most to be
pitied" (1 Corinthians 15:14, 17, 19). The worst attitude
toward death that one can possibly have is to try to ignore its reality. Michael Green says, "It is not in the least
fortuitous that in our day the rise of atheistic humanism
should have coincided with the decline of religion and
the increasing attempt to brush the ugly fact of death
under the carpet."

To find meaning in what we do we must be sure that
our work will abide. This assurance can be ours if we
believe in the resurrection. At the end of the great
chapter on the resurrection, and after that outburst of
triumph, "O death, where is thy victory?" Paul concludes: "Therefore, my beloved brethren, be steadfast,
immovable, always abounding in the work of the Lord,
knowing that in the Lord your labor is not in vain."

Not only are our labors not futile if Christ is alive, but our sufferings also take on meaning. If death were the end of it all, we would not risk our lives for the sake of Christ. We would not waste our energies seeking to build His kingdom. Paul, writing about his sufferings in Asia, says, "We felt that we had received the sentence of death; but that was to make us rely not on ourselves but on God who raises the dead" (2 Corinthians 1:9). A bit later, in the same letter, he confesses that, although death works in his life, he does not cease to speak the good news, "knowing that he who raised the Lord Jesus will raise us also with Jesus" (4:14). The cry of the innocent martyrs is, "O Sovereign Lord, holy and true, how long?" (Revelation 6:10). The answer comes back, "Wait just a little longer. Your suffering is not meaningless; God will yet redress the wrongs done to you."

Before Dietrich Bonhoeffer was led to his death by Hitler's guards, he spoke to the prisoners on the text, "Blessed be the God and Father of our Lord Jesus Christ! By his great mercy we have been born anew to a living hope through the resurrection of Jesus Christ from the dead" (1 Peter 1:3). And as they took him away, he sent this last message to the Bishop of Chichester, "This is the end—but for me the beginning of life."

Take away the resurrection and the foundation for Christian ethics also crumbles, and all efforts to do right are vain. Why should we try to live upright and godly lives if death ends everything? "If the dead are not raised, 'Let us eat and drink, for tomorrow we die' " (1 Corinthians 15:32). In the second century *Apology of Anthenagoras*, we read: "Were we convinced that this life is the only one, then we might be suspected of sinning, by being enslaved to flesh and blood and by becoming subject to gain and lust. But since we realize that God is a witness, day and night, of our thoughts and our speech, and that by being pure light, He can see into our very hearts, we are convinced that when we depart this present life we shall live another. . . . In the light of this it is not likely that we would be purposely wicked, and deliver ourselves up to the great Judge to be punished."

4. Conclusion

The resurrection is the answer to our guilt, our loneliness, and to the feeling of futility. This is what makes the gospel of the resurrection so relevant, so vital, so meaningful. It is not enough to confess that Christ rose from the dead two millennia ago. Nor is it sufficient that the church acknowledges its faith in the resurrection annually during the great Easter festival. We must, as Paul suggests, "celebrate the festival" daily (1 Corinthians 5:8). And how do we do this? By finding meaning in our daily tasks which we do in Christ's name (they are not futile). By practicing the presence of the risen Lord in our daily life (we are not alone). By rejoicing in the deep assurance of sins forgiven (our guilt is gone).

Risen with Christ

Dr. W. B. Hinson *was told he had one year at most to live. It was Easter season. He entered his pulpit and preached a sermon of confidence and assurance. He said:*

"From my house I looked across at the nearby mountains and the river. I looked at the stately trees. Then, when night came, I looked into the sky where God was lighting His lamps. I said, 'I may not see you many more times, but mountains, I shall be alive when you are gone. River, I shall be alive when you cease running to the sea. Stars, I shall be alive when you have fallen from your sockets in the great downward pull of the material universe.' "

*This is the confidence of resurrection. Christ's resurrection is the pledge of our resurrection. When Effie Jane Wheeler, who served for sixteen years on the Wheaton College faculty, was told she was dying, she replied, "I do not give a cold good-bye but rather a warm **auf Wiedersehen,** till I see you again."*

—John M. Drescher

20

RISEN WITH CHRIST

By John R. Mumaw

If then you have been raised with Christ, seek the things that are above. Colossians 3:1.

An old Roman once tried to make a corpse stand on its feet by bracing it with props. After many futile attempts he gave up, saying, "There is something missing inside."[1] What the body needed was not props, but a new life. So it is with man; he needs more than a reasonable philosophy of life or a belief in correct doctrine. He needs the recurring restoration of an inner dynamic. This will produce "love, joy, peace, patience, kindness, goodness, faithfulness, gentleness, self-control" (Galatians 5:22, 23). This is the resurrection life.

1. Resurrection Life Engages Human Dimensions

(a) It is an unfolding life. God looks upon the believer not only as having been raised in his saving experience

---

John R. Mumaw, Harrisonburg, Virginia, has held numerous churchwide posts including moderator of the Mennonite Church and editor of *The Christian Ministry.* He was professor of Christian education and president of Eastern Mennonite College, Harrisonburg, Virginia, from 1948 to 1965.

with Christ but also as being in need of progressive moral improvement. It is not enough to have faith. The Christian must grow in his likeness to Christ. Christianity is more than a world-view; it is the experience of God in the ordinary affairs of men.

The resurrection life begins with being united to Christ when one enters into a participation of eternal life with Him. The resurrection walk begins at the same time. Since we are risen with Christ (Colossians 2:12), we must anticipate and demonstrate behavior that expresses the nature of eternal life. "It goes on unfolding and developing itself before our death, and after our death, until at last, in the most exact and full sense, as to our whole person, body as well as soul, the resurrection of Christ becomes ours."[2] In the meantime we are in the process of being changed from one step of moral quality to a higher and yet higher level, reaching after the image of Christ (2 Corinthians 3:18). The death to self and the resurrection to life in the individual believer is only the beginning of a process in which moral behavior is being molded after a pattern of divine ideals.

(b) It is a progressive life. The unfolding of Christ's own character within the believer's life forms a pattern of behavior that relates the New Testament ethic to contemporary living. Christianity is a force that can adopt and refashion and assimilate the most diverse cultural elements into a practicing faith that forms a single basis of moral responsibility.[3] Herein lies the secret of its permanent character and living power. John presents Jesus as the One who confers life-giving power to those who believe. He wrote from the viewpoint of resurrection faith and the prospect of resurrection power. Let us pray that we too might know the power of His

resurrection (Philippians 3:10-12).

(c) It is a committed life. Although human nature pulls the believer toward death, faith in the resurrection draws upward and onward toward eternal life. The idea of justification grows in meaning and broadens in application. Jesus lived for us and died in our place; God raised Him on our behalf that He might live for us again and forever.

The Anabaptists pressed the doctrine of justification to the point of its moral implication. For them to live in the state of justification was to "walk in the resurrection." They had a sense of a growing personal commitment to the One who justifies. They did not depend on the merits of good works to justify their sins, but held to faith as a means to secure salvation. They distinguished sharply between "works of merit" and "works of faith" giving due emphasis upon justification by faith along with their insistence upon holy living.

Faith in the resurrection of Christ as a matter of fact and as a matter of doctrine is basic to this resurrection walk. As a historic event it constitutes the basis of the new life in Christ. The significance of its meaning has relevance to living. "Therefore, since we are justified by faith, we have peace with God" (Romans 5:1). God is acting toward us as He did toward Christ, treating us now precisely as he treated Him in the resurrection glory.

(d) It is a conferred life. Regeneration is best viewed in the context of a personal encounter with the risen Christ. "Once the Spirit of him who raised Jesus from the dead lives within you He will, by that same Spirit, bring to your whole being new strength and vitality" (Romans 8:11, Phillips). A sense of having been remade within and of having received a new moral power enables the believer to make courageous decisions. "It is when we go

beyond the idea, the language, the theology of regeneration, into the experience of a conferred life—nothing less
than the impartation of the very life of God—that this offer of the gospel makes sense."[4]

The New Testament emphasis on holy living assumes
and requires a new birth. The body of sin derived from
the first birth must be mortified, with all its lustful
desires, so as to be able to walk in newness of life. All who
have been "changed in mind and disposition through the
eternal saving seed of God (1 Peter 1:23) should be
godly, and heavenly-minded, and yearn for and desire
heavenly, incorruptible things."[5]

When Christ gains access to the human heart He pours
into it "the power of an endless life." This timeless life
with God brings to human behavior high moral and
spiritual qualities. Christianity has a creed to be
believed, but it is more essentially a life to be lived.[6]
Apart from the risen Savior the creed is an empty form.
Confession of creed must be related to a conferred life.
The moral dynamics of the new birth expand from within
and produce new motives, new habits, a new outlook,
and new desires. One becomes engaged in new activities
and moves toward new goals.

When Saul met Christ on the Damascus road, he was
confronted directly by a living Person. It was not so
much what Saul heard and saw that convinced him of his
own need, but the existence of the risen Savior and what
he understood Him to be. "It was the Saviour's personality borne in upon Paul's consciousness which led
him for the first time to relent in his policy of persecution, and to perceive how erroneous it had been, and how
needful it now was to surrender to this new-found
Lord."[7] That surrender was the secret of a new life and

the motivation of new behavior. He acted in personal response to the call of Christ and found for his own life the freedom of Christian liberty.

2. Resurrection Life Has Eternal Dimensions

When Jesus said, "I am the resurrection and the life," He spoke to the point of a present reality. His giving life to the world (John 6:33-35) and the believer's receiving eternal life (John 5:24) are one and the same in the experience of salvation. Life lived in the power and the reality of the resurrection puts off the self-life and puts on the Christ-life. "There can be no advance in the spiritual life, no power in testimony, no effective pleading in prayer, no advance in grace, and no initiation into the secrets of God, till there is abandonment of the whole life of self."[8]

(a) It is living in the light of God. "If we walk in the light, as he is in the light, we have fellowship with one another, and the blood of Jesus Christ his Son cleanses us from all sin" (1 John 1:7). To know that the process of cleansing continues to be effective has moral value. One who is committed to "walk in the light" is thereby privileged to walk in the power of the resurrection. In this sense the believer participates in the resurrection daily.

(b) It is living in union with Christ. The resurrection of Christ is both the pledge and the dynamic of eternal life. As a pledge it assures the believer that the final sacrifice in Christ's dying was sufficient to expiate all human sin. The dynamic of His resurrection resides in the fact that he was placed in a position where He could keep in constant contact with the lives He had redeemed.[9] "For those sharing in the resurrection experience the fruits of

the kingdom are already begun. The church has become the vehicle of eternity coming into time, the result of Jesus' resurrection being a continuing personal experience."[10] His continued sharing of that life with the believer is the creative force that provides moral vitality for living. The constant awareness of His pulsating presence produces courage to do and dare in kingdom affairs.

(c) *It is living in the light of eternity.* Eternal life is sharing the life of God not on the basis of promise for the future, but precisely as a present possession. It views the obligations of life in the light of eternity. It is a practical awareness of belonging now to the eternal world. "The eternal world, however, does not stand in such an exclusive relation to the temporal world in which we live, that we must leave this world behind before we can participate in the eternal. On the contrary, it is of the nature of piety to seek the traces of the eternal in everything that is and happens."[11] The resurrection of Christ has brought to earth the most evident trace of eternity. Therein is demonstrated the quality of experience that belongs to the sphere of the eternal.

3. Resurrection Life Anticipates the Consummation

God wants to share with man His own blessedness. As Creator He longs to see His creatures happy. As Father He wants His children to love Him. As sovereign Judge He looks for gratitude from those to whom He shows mercy. He looks beyond the confines of human and temporal expressions to divine and eternal values. This is the goal of redemption. It will be achieved finally in the bodily resurrection of the saints.

(a) *It is living with a divine promise.* Reference to the

redeeming act of God as a means of salvation takes into consideration spirit, soul, and body. "God created man as a whole and therefore as a whole He will redeem him."[12] No part of man will remain in death. "Death is swallowed up in victory" (1 Corinthians 15:54). The consummating act of redemption will be a bodily resurrection. Christ looked upon this as a special part of His work, for He said, "No one can come to me unless the Father who sent me draws him; and I will raise him up at the last day" (John 6:44). "He who eats my flesh and drinks my blood has eternal life, and I will raise him up at the last day" (John 6:54).

(b) It is living with the Spirit pledge. The indwelling of the Holy Spirit is a pledge of the resurrection. This present experience of resurrection power is a foretaste of what is promised. The consummation of our redemption is yet to come. We look toward this future event as the final answer to the struggle against the corrupting elements of sin. Christ will triumph over all evil. "And not only the creatures, but we ourselves, who have the first fruits of the Spirit, groan inwardly as we wait for adoption as sons, with redemption of our bodies" (Romans 8:23). This mortal body shall be touched, raised, and changed. The Lord Jesus Christ at His second coming "will remake these wretched bodies of ours to resemble his own glorious body" (Philippians 3:21, Phillips).

The resurrection hope is intelligible only on the basis of understanding the close relation between the past, present, and future aspects of resurrection truth. The New Testament establishes a close connection between faith in the already realized resurrection of Christ, faith in the present work of the resurrection power, and faith in the promise of the future resurrection. "Because we, on the basis of the resurrection of Christ and by faith in this redemptive fact, are able in the present to gain possession of the Holy Spirit, we know that we may hope for the resurrection of the body, which is effected through the same Spirit who already dwells in us."[13] "If the Spirit of him who raised Jesus from the dead dwells in you, he who raised Christ Jesus from the dead will give life to your mortal bodies also through his Spirit which dwells in you" (Romans 8:11).

(c) It is living with a blessed hope. The hope that dwells in the heart of the true believer holds to the promises that in the future all will be restored to the original pattern of holiness. This hope itself is a part of the saving process, for "in this hope we were saved" (Romans 8:24). Having been born to a living hope, we look to the power of God to guard us through our faith for "a salvation ready to be revealed in the last time" (1 Peter 1:5). This hope sees by anticipation the salvation which is to be completed then.[14] The great final resurrection of the body is only an extension of having been raised from the death of sin to newness of life. The redeemed sinner who has undergone this radical change is in process of preparation to pass through another change, the transformation into a heavenly life.

The Christian faith is based on a special revelation from God. This means the believer accepts certain things from the Bible as truth that would otherwise be unknown. He knows something about the nature of life after death because he believes what the Bible says about it. We know Christ is risen: therefore we have faith in the promise of our own resurrection and have the kind of hope which has for its object the pardon, the favor, the approval, and the love of God. The Christian hope is well-founded on the Word of promise and the testimony of experience to give present peace and pure joy in God. Beyond the eternal life of the present we also cherish the thought of what we are to experience in the future.

"Faith is a spiritual quality in men that leads them to believe that there is a future life as well as a future death and constrains them to do something about it. Those who have faith are led to choose and to practice those things that strengthen and develop the spiritual life and to make preparations for the promised life beyond."[15] This kind of hope serves to keep the soul anchored to the heavenly goal. We know that whatever happened in Christ's resurrection from the dead will happen in ours.

(d) It is living on resurrection ground. We are now saved from the wrath to come (1 Thessalonians 1:10) and have hope to enter the glories of heaven. We are being saved from the power of Satan and sin (Ephesians 6:11) and look forward to being delivered from the very presence of evil. God has placed us on resurrection ground. By the power of Christ's resurrection we can overcome every enemy and be saved from all failures and defeat.[16] But we look for a Savior whose coming will precipitate a resurrection of the saints (Philippians 3:20, 21), and complete the salvation of all the redeemed (Hebrews 9:28). It is to this that we are begotten and kept by the power of God through faith unto salvation to be revealed in the last time (1 Peter 1:5).

The apostolic church lived and served in the midst of intense persecution and suffering. It treated the doctrine of the resurrection as something more than a creed to be accepted; to the early Christians it was the basis of personal hope. The resurrection meant to them that in the end the power that raised Jesus from the dead would also raise us up with glorified bodies.

(e) *It anticipates a final restoration.* Redemptive history will close its course with the end-time events. In view of the purpose of God in creation, of His power to accomplish His purposes, of the far-reaching effects of redemption to save the whole man and to renovate the whole earth, and of the completeness of His sovereignty which He shall establish[17] we look for a resurrected body to enjoy the new heaven and the new earth. Accordingly the resurrection of the body continues to be reserved for the future consummation of all things.

Faith in the risen and living Lord is related to both present experience and future event. Belief in the final consummation gave meaning to the whole course of human history because it makes sense out of human being. It has the vision of ultimate triumph. God will yet have His purpose fulfilled.

If Christ had not risen we would have no hope and the Christian dead would have perished. But now is Christ risen from the dead and become the forerunner of that final event toward which all creation moves. This not only proves that the dead can be raised, but it is a promise that they will be raised. Christ was the first to reverse the trend of disobedience. He has turned the supreme tragedy of the race to a final triumph of the redemptive purpose. The open tomb indicates that Christ passed through the ordeal of death victoriously and took away its "sting." He overcame the limitations of this life and introduced the life to come. His resurrection was the preamble of ours. "What has happened with Him is a preview of what shall take place in the final restoration of all things."[18]

1. Merrill C. Tenny, *Resurrection Realities* (Bible House, 1945), p. 53.

2. Robert S. Candlish, *Life in a Risen Saviour* (Adam & Black, 1863), p. 125.

3. Andres Nygren, *The Essence of Christianity* (Muhlenberg, 1961), p. 62.

4. Claude H. Thompson, *The Theology of the Kerygma* (Prentice-Hall, 1962), p. 136.

5. Menno Simons, *The Complete Writings of Menno Simons* (Herald Press, 1950), p. 58.

6. Walter R. Martin, *Essential Christianity* (Zondervan, 1962), p. 56.

7. R. M'Cheyne Edgar, *Gospel of a Risen Saviour* (T & T Clark, 1892), p. 59.

8. F. E. Marsh, *What Does the Resurrection of Christ Mean?* (Bass & Co., n.d.), p. 150.

9. Merrill C. Tenny, *Reality of Resurrection* (Harper & Row, 1963), p. 70.

10. Thomas S. Kepler, *The Meaning and Mystery of the Resurrection* (Association Press, 1963), p. 142.

11. Nygren, *op. cit.*, p. 28.

12. Eric Saver, *The Triumph of the Crucified* (Eerdmans, 1955), p. 106.

13. Oscar Cullman, *Christ and Time* (Westminster, 1950), p. 237.

14. Theodore R. Clark, *Saved by His Life* (Macmillan, 1959), p. 210.

15. George N. Mendenhall, *Basic Teachings of the New Testament* (Vantage, 1962), p. 144.

16. F. E. Marsh, *op. cit.*, p. 203.

17. Paul Erb, *The Alpha and Omega* (Herald Press, 1955), p. 120.

18. Erie H. Wahlstrom, *God Who Redeems* (Muhlenberg, 1962), p. 128.

The Conquering Lamb

One of the hymns of Charles Wesley, *not as well known as it might be, is entitled "Surrounded by a Host of Foes." It contains a meaningful verse of defiant hope and courage:*

> *What tho' a thousand hosts engage,*
> *A thousand worlds, my soul to shake?*
> *I have a shield shall quell their rage,*
> *And drive the alien armies back;*
> *Portray'd it bears a bleeding Lamb:*
> *I dare believe in Jesus' name.*

Behold, the Lamb of God, who takes away the sin of the world! John 1:29.

You know that you were ransomed . . . not with perishable things such as silver or gold, but with the precious blood of Christ, like that of a Lamb without blemish or spot. 1 Peter 1:18, 19.

21
THE CONQUERING LAMB
By Donald R. Jacobs

*To him who sits upon the throne and to the Lamb be bless-
ing and honor and glory and might for ever and ever! Revelation 5:13.*

The year is 1977, a tyrannical ruler, Idi Amin, is vent-
ing his wrath on the suffering church in Uganda, not unlike the infamous Nero whose swords butchered innocent
followers of Jesus in the first century. In a moment of
uncontrolled hate Amin put to death the Anglican
archbishop, Janani Luwum, on false charges. The church
was stunned. They had already seen their pews emptied
of some of their gifted men. Widows and orphans
increased in the churches, striking evidence of the
systematic slaughter of the leaders in Christian communities. When and how was it all to stop? Is there no

Donald R. Jacobs, Landisville, Pennsylvania, served for many years as edu-
ator and bishop in Tanzania, Africa, and in the United States. He was the
founder and principal of Mennonite Theological College, Musoma, Tanzania.
At present he is executive director of Mennonite Christian Leadership Foundation and overseas secretary for the Eastern Mennonite Board of Missions,
Salunga, Pennsylvania.

answer, they must have surely thought, to the fierce rage of men? Has God turned His back?

In moments of extremity like this, when the church sees those who are strong in faith falling victim to the cruel sword of persecution, they frame the question, as did the church in Uganda, "How can One who hung on a cross, who couldn't even drive away a fly from His face, be the power of God?" Paul states the fact clearly in 1 Corinthians 1:23, 24 where he insists that Jesus Christ crucified is the power of God. If so, then why does He seem so powerless, especially when it is obvious that His people are undergoing extreme persecution? Can He not break the sword?

I remember my confusion when, a decade ago, I received the sad news that a dear Kenya brother had died of wounds inflicted when he refused to take the tribal blood oath. He told the others that he already had drunk the blood of God's Lamb and any other blood oath would not mix with that. In a rage the others beat him mercilessly. As we buried his body on the side of a Kikuyu hill, we too were brought to the moment of questions. Why does God allow these beautiful disciples of Jesus Christ to die while their killers sit back in satisfaction? Why does the power of God seem so weak at times in face of the terrible wrath and force of evil men?

These very questions must have circled the head of John the Revelator like pesky flies, for he, too, saw the sword of power decimate the little communities of faith. This iron hand grasped even him with its terrible power and banished him to an island in the sea. It was while he was in this state of confusion that God graciously granted him the clear revelation of the wonderful ways of suffering love (Revelation 4 and 5).

1. Lion or Lamb?

It was the Lord's day, a time to meditate, a time to open one's heart, in a special way to the mind of God. John saw God on His throne, an encouragement in itself, I suspect. God had not been dethroned nor had he abdicated. He was still the ruler of heaven and earth. But how does He rule? What are His weapons? Where are His armies? John must have thought of a dozen such questions.

The answers began to unfold. The book containing the divine mystery, sealed with seven heavy seals, appeared in the hands of God who sat in regal splendor on His throne. John realized that that book held the answers to the questions of a suffering church. He waited in keen anticipation for the book to be opened. Then an angel with a loud voice cried out, "Who is worthy to open the book?" The question echoes through the universe and died in silence. No man was able to open the book. It remained closed.

John, bitterly disappointed, wept. One of the elders, seeing John's anxiety, whispered to him the good news. "Look carefully" he said. "See the Lion of the tribe of Judah, the Root of David? He can do it."

And so John waited for the Lion, the symbol of power and authority who with a snarl and swipe of a fierce paw would make short work of the seals. He could scarcely wait to hear the mighty roar of overwhelming strength, to see with what ease the Lion would take the seals and rip them apart.

Wait, John, the way the book is opened is crucially important. Pay careful attention, John, to God's way. Then John's eyes were arrested by something he had not really seen for all of the splendor of light and singing. There, standing before the throne, among the twenty-four elders, was a Lamb who wore the crimson scar of death on its throat. It was the symbol of utter weakness, a sacrificial Lamb whose life had been drained completely. Instead of a Lion there stood a sacrificial Lamb.

As he pondered this extraordinary vision perhaps John's mind flashed back a few years when the crowd cried "Hosanna, Hosanna" as Jesus rode the colt into Jerusalem. They saw him as the conquering Lion of the tribe of Judah who was about to establish the kingdom of God on earth with power and glory. The Lion is coming, they thought. But a few days later Jesus hung limp and dead on a criminal's cross wearing the scars of death in His body. Who could have seen in that spent, poured-out life the hope of all creation? That battered frame looked so futile, so utterly hopeless, just as hopeless as the little Lamb standing among the elders in heaven. What could the Lamb do that no man could do?

In a moment that blessed Lamb moved forward, took the book, and with ease opened its seals. "He can do it," the elders cried out, and the angels quickly joined the choir of thanksgiving. The Worthy One was found who could take the book, and open its seals. I think the emphasis must be on the "one" for no other could do it, not the plural bloods of bulls and goats and sheep, but the poured-out life of God in the flesh, Jesus Christ the Righteous.

A new song filled heaven. "Worthy art thou . . . for thou wast slain and by thy blood didst ransom men for God from every tribe and tongue and people and nation, and hast made them a kingdom and priests to our God."

It was little wonder that the hosts of heaven joined the cosmic chorus, accompanied by every living thing in heaven and on the earth and under the earth and in the sea in that final song of redemption. "To him who sits upon the throne and to the Lamb be blessing and honor and glory and might for ever and ever!"

2. Power or Weakness?

As John witnessed the power of the Lamb he saw Christ crucified who in the eyes of carnal man was despised and rejected, a Person to be pitied, perhaps, but certainly not worshiped. For who can worship weakness? Man worships power. This carpenter's son, while hanging on the cross could not chase a fly from His face. That is what the crowd saw. But John now sees what carnal man cannot see, that this Jesus of Nazareth was none other than the eternal Lamb of God who alone had the power to open the book.

John's Hebrew background flashed on his mind. The Bible scarcely opens when God is seen slaying an innocent animal to make clothing for Adam and Eve. They had gotten into trouble of the worst kind. They said "no" to God, and a train of events followed which impaired almost every aspect of their lives, including their relationship to one another.

Previous to this their nakedness was not a problem, but when they lifted themselves up as challengers of the divine wisdom they focused attention on their own egos and discovered that they were terribly undone. They quickly invented temporary, almost absurd, solutions—fig leaf clothes.

God soon saw the futility of it and in His love He walked among His innocent animals, selecting one or so for slaughter, the innocent for the guilty, the sinless for the sinful, the obedient for the disobedient. The poor creature yielded its own precious life so that the sinning persons could live comfortably with God and with one another. And so it was that the first sacrificial blood was spilled.

When our primal parents saw that pool of innocent blood on the green earth, a life given completely for them, they probably felt a pang of pity for that animal and a moment of thanksgiving. As they covered their nakedness with the skin of "another" they realized that they were recipients of grace, the loving grace of God and the substitutionary grace of the self-giving creature. I like to think that the first sacrifice was a lamb.

When the plague of death swept Egypt God's people were again in trouble and the answer was much the same, an innocent animal, a lamb or a kid, whose life was given because of man's weakness. They were directed to kill a lamb for each household and place the blood on the doorposts. The poured-out life of "another" was their covering.

In every transaction between man and God the awful effects of man's frailty, his utter inability to compensate for his persistent disobedience, emerges as the critical factor. It is not enough simply to acknowledge God as God and to try to please Him with good works or appease Him by claiming that we are not really all that delinquent. We know in the inner chambers of our consciousness that we need a Lamb, a pure life, to be poured out so that it can cover our own.

At the center of the man-God encounter is suffering, pain, and death because of the very nature of man's helplessness. Try to avoid this as we may, the truth will out, we need the covering of a holy life in order to have relaxed communion with our Creator and with our fellow creatures. We need a sacrificial Lamb to empower us for godly living.

The Jews, like most of mankind, slaughtered animals by the hundreds of thousands because of this fundamental need, but always realized that the animals are not really effective sacrifices because they lack the freedom, intelligence, and personality of people.

3. Suffering Servant

Isaiah caught this clearly in his prophetic vision when he saw the Suffering Servant going "as a lamb to the slaughter," a human being, not an animal who could carry the iniquity of all persons in His own body. This Suffering Servant was none other than God in the flesh, Jesus Christ of Nazareth.

John paused in his baptizing. The moment he had anticipated had arrived. Before him stood Jesus requesting baptism. John turned to the congregation of people gathered at Jordan and announced with joy and pathos, "Look. He is God's Lamb."

Jesus suffered as a Lamb and He died as a Lamb who "before his shearers is dumb." Jesus made it abundantly clear that sin, man's innate inability to align his will with the revealed will of God, is without human remedy. It requires for its solution divine initiative and divine suffering.

Those who follow the Jesus way acknowledge this freely and gladly admit that their relationship with God is made possible only because Jesus has become their covering. Their lives demonstrate this fact. They attempt so to live in Christ through repentant faith that the very mind of Christ gives them a new nature, a nature which does not seek to avoid the cross and suffering for the sake of some illusive happiness, but they take up their cross daily with gladness. They experience in similar proportions both pathos and joy. They discover that Jesus' suffering did not make their own unnecessary but the presence of Jesus gives them the courage to walk through suffering, just like Jesus did.

The cross remains the central focus of Christian faith. The startling fact is not that Jesus rose from the dead— we could expect this of the Incarnate God—but who could have predicted His death? That is the eternal mystery. Why did God in Christ die? He died, very simply, so that we might live.

Again it is 1977 in Uganda. The sword of force meets the power of the love of God and for a moment it appears as though God is helpless. But He is there, in His suffering servants. Festo Kivengere, a witness to this mystery, writes, "How can One who hung on a cross, who couldn't even drive a fly from His face, be the power of God? Because in love He prayed for the men who drove the nails into His hands to kill Him, 'Father, forgive these men, they don't understand!'

"He who hung on the cross in blood and sweat is the One who can embrace humanity, change, and re-create it. I know, because one day I opened my poor heart to Jesus Christ, and the cross did a miracle. God set me free, sending me through the fields to ask people's forgiveness. I remember the day I bicycled fifty miles to a white man whom I had hated. I stood there in his house, telling him what Christ had done for me, and that now I was free and saw him as my brother. English as he was, he stood there weeping, and we were in each other's arms. I used no weapon, but Christ's love had won. This is victory! This is the power which the world is desperately in need of" (*I Loved Idi Amin*, Revell, 1977). This story is also our story.

4. *Power to Change Life*

The greatest power on earth is the power which can make a friend of an enemy. Force deals with enemies by destroying them. But the destruction of enemies is nothing less than the admission of utter powerlessness. The power of the Lamb is the power to change lives. We are inclined to think that the greatest exhibition of power is the power to preserve life. This is not so, the greatest exhibition of power is the power to change life, to turn from self-worship to loving submission to the loving Father.

When Jesus hung on the cross, it is true, He could not chase a fly from his bleeding brow. But He was forgiving men and women of their sins. He was bearing in His body man's iniquity so that He might change them. The greatest power is the power of Calvary love.

Paul comprehended this. He was racing toward Damascus with the power of the Sanhedrin in his hand and the power of hate and misguided zeal in his heart. Speaking as a human he was power-laden. But on that road he met the greatest power of all before whom his swords and affidavits and hates were useless. He met Jesus Christ of Nazareth. He met Calvary love and it changed his life.

What of God's precious martyrs? Did He desert them? What of us when we feel that evil men are overpowering the church? This is only in appearances. The power of the witness of Janani Luwum, of the Kikuyu brother, of all who suffer lovingly for Christ's sake is greater than the combined swords of men because they have in their breasts the divine power of a changed life. This power which flows from the cross of Jesus Christ has no equal.

The Apostle John sees it ever so clearly, the way of the Lamb is the power of God, for in Him is sacrificial love fulfilled. This Lamb has captured us. His love overpowered us. Now Jesus goes about lovingly transforming our lionlike natures into lamblike natures. Reviled, we smile; threatened, we threaten not; hated, we love; killed, we give life; made poor, we own the earth. This is the miracle of the living presence of the Lamb of God in our hearts.

The Immortal Christ

Benjamin Franklin *wrote the epitaph that appeared on his tomb:*

The Body of
Benjamin Franklin
(Like the Cover of an Old Book,
Its contents torn out
And Stript of its Lettering and Gilding)
Lies Here, Food for Worms
Yet the Work Itself Shall Not Be Lost,
for It Will (as He Believed) Appear Once More
In a New
And More Beautiful Edition
Corrected and Amended
by
the Author

22

THE IMMORTAL CHRIST
By Paul Erb

"I am the Alpha and the Omega," says the Lord God, who is and who was and who is to come, the Almighty. Revelation 1:8.

Dr. R. W. Dale, an English preacher, was deep in the preparation of an Easter sermon when the thought of a living Christ broke in upon him as never before.

"Christ is alive," he said to himself, "Alive!" After a pause he said again, "Alive! Can that really be true? Living as really as I myself am?" He got up and walked about repeating, "Christ is living! Christ is living!"

At first it seemed strange and hardly true, but at last it came upon him like a burst of sudden glory: "Yes, Christ is living now." He thought he had believed this all along. But not until that moment did he feel so sure in his faith.

"My people shall know about it; I shall preach this

Paul Erb, Scottdale, Pennsylvania, was professor of English at Goshen College, Goshen, Indiana, held pastorates in a number of states, and was for seventeen years editor of the *Gospel Herald*, the official weekly of the Mennonite Church. He is author of *Bible Prophecy: Questions and Answers* (Herald Press, 1978).

great truth again and again until they believe it as I do now." For months afterward, and in every sermon, the living Christ was Dale's one great theme. And Carr's Lane became known as the church where they sang an Easter hymn every Sunday. When a visitor asked why they sang an Easter hymn on a November Sunday morning, Dr. Dale explained: "We want to celebrate the glorious fact that Christ is alive; and Sunday is the day that He left the grave" (*Anthology of Jesus*, Harper and Brothers, 1926).

In Revelation 1:8 Jesus Christ, the "Lord God," describes Himself as the one "who is and who was and who is to come." And in verse 18 this timeless One says He is "the Living one" who "was dead, and behold, I am alive for evermore" (ASV). Evidently the immortal Christ cannot be limited by grammatical tenses or other categories of time, which has a beginning and an ending. William H. Hudnit, Jr., in *The Life of Christ in Poetry* (Association Press, 1957) wrote:

> Christ was no prisoner of time,
>   His truth transcends each age;
> His words beyond compare, sublime,
>   His life, death's endless page."

1. Christ Was

The full dynamic of Christ, it is true, is realized in eternity, not in time. But the stupendous drama of redemption, in which God chose Him to be the central character, has its acts and scenes, its dated moments of beginnings and endings. These dates have to do with the past, the present, and the future of human history. It is the will of the Godhead that within history this drama of divine action should accomplish redemption for mankind, cancel the effects of man's sin, and restore peace and order into the chaos which Satan has caused.

The immortal Christ was involved in the beginnings of history. John tells that the Word, another name for Christ, was in the beginning with God, and that all things were made through Him. Paul wrote to the Colossians that in Him were all things created, whether the nonhuman nature of things that we see, or the human race of mankind.

Also in the past is the commitment of Christ to devote Himself to the Father's plan for man's redemption. He was willing to come to earth and take upon Himself the limitations of a human body. He took up the burden of incarnation, going the way of suffering and death on the cross. His whole incarnational ministry was written into the sacred history of salvation: His teaching, His crucifixion, His resurrection, and His ascension again to the Father. All this is the good news of what happened in history at the high moment of revelation in which God was at work in making and writing into performance a plan for salvation through the immortal Christ.

The highest point, the climax of what Christ experienced in the past, is His resurrection from the dead. In it He triumphed over sin and all the wicked purposes of Satan and his hosts. For now it had been demonstrated that evil and death were only temporary, that God had set their limits. The very heart of what we believe and teach is that Jesus' grave could not hold Him. He died on the cross to save us. But there is efficacy in that death only because He is now alive. We have a living Savior!

When His ministry on earth was completed, Christ ascended to the Father. His saving function continues at God's right hand, where He intercedes for us. The ascension convinced the disciples that, generally speaking, the appearances of the resurrected Jesus were at an end. However, there were two significant appearances after the ascension. One was on the Damascus Road, where Saul was convinced of the reality of a living Lord. The other is the setting of our text in Revelation 1. There John is assured that Christ is alive.

2. *Christ Is*

The present reality of the living Christ is the ministry of the Holy Spirit in every true believer. Beginning at Pentecost the Spirit is given to those who by faith open their hearts to Him. For the Spirit is of the same Godhead as Christ is, and as the Spirit works in us, Christ Himself is alive in us. He is our Teacher and Guide, our empowerment and the source of Spirit fruit and gifts. But primarily it is the work of the Spirit to exalt Christ and interpret His work of salvation. The moving of the Spirit witnesses to the immortal Christ.

Paul wrote to the Galatians that he is crucified with Christ. But, he says, "Christ . . . liveth in me; and the life I now live in the flesh I live by faith in the Son of God." The phrase, "Christ in me," and its parallel, "in Christ," is used by Paul several hundred times. This is the way the great apostle described the supernatural relationship which he had with the living Christ. How could he deny that Christ is immortal? Paul knew in his daily experience what it is to be engrafted in fellowship and union with Christ. As we are in the air and the air in us, so we are in Christ and Christ in us. Or as water is in a sponge and the sponge in the water, so are we in conscious communion with Him.

This is both an individual and corporate matter, as the

Spirit-Christ indwells His body, the church. Believers are in Christ, and Christ is in His people.

This is a present, a convincing, a joyous reality. As one of our gospel songs goes,

> Christ liveth in me,
>   Christ liveth in me;
> Oh, what a salvation this,
>   That Christ liveth in me.

Such an experience cannot be limited to earthly time. It is possible only because Christ came and brought in a new age; He created a new humanity. Though we are still in the old age, we are in Christ a new order, created in Christ to a new kind of existence. The old and the new overlap. We are still in the old world, but living there a new life. "At Ephesus" but also "in Christ." The old age has not yet gone, but the new age has already come. This is the blessed paradox: already, but not yet. The eschatology which will some day unfold in complete fulfillment is already in process. Some day, but not yet, we shall be with Him in eternal glory. Already He is with us in the life and power of His resurrection.

3. Christ Is to Come

The immortal Christ who was and is, is yet to come—the coming One. This future is what many people think prophecy is all about. Actually the future gets its meaning only from what the ever-living Lord Jesus has already done and what He is doing now. What was foretold by Old Testament prophets began to be fulfilled in Christ's first coming. He did accomplish redemption upon the cross and on resurrection morning. He laid the foundations of a believing church, and after He had gone back

to His Father, he sent forth the Spirit at Pentecost. But
there was much in the messianic promise that was fully
given. This was the subject of apostolic preaching.

Jesus told His disciples He must come again. He did
not tell them when He would come. His coming He
described as the Parousia, or the presence. This Parousia
would be the opening event of what he had yet to do. Almost every writer of the New Testament books mentions
this coming, the last day, the day of Christ.

It will be, indeed, the day of the Lord. The focus of
revelation will be on Jesus Christ. It once was and now is
on His death and resurrection power. It will be on Him
as He comes in light and power and great glory. This will
be the time of His apocalypse, His unveiling, a breaking
into history of the glory of God. This will be the revelation to the world of Jesus as Lord.

The immortality of Christ will then be seen in the full
flowering of what He called "eternal (everlasting) life."
When He was here it was given unto Him "to have life in
Himself." In Him eternal life appeared in the midst of
history. He offered Himself as the life. This is not the life
of days and years, but of timeless eternity. It is the
harvest of unending life offered to all who will partake.

One of the accompaniments of the Parousia is the
resurrection—not the resurrection of Christ, for that is
past—but the end-time resurrection, when all who are in
their graves shall come forth. Because Christ the Immortal arose as the firstfruits of the resurrection, so we
too shall experience a rising from the dead.

Another thing we shall share with the immortal Christ
is His glory—the glory which shall be revealed (1 Peter
5:1). Then shall He appear as He really is, the Lord of
glory. And we shall be manifested with Him in glory

(Colossians 3:4). We shall help to reflect His glory. Who would want to miss that experience? When the three disciples saw and heard on the Mount of Transfiguration what must have been a mere foretaste of the eternal glory, they wanted to make shelters and stay there. The immortal Christ was sharing a bit of heavenly communication with them. What will be the fullness of that resplendent glory!

Having known here the blessedness of the first beginnings of redemption and salvation, it is good to see throughout the whole New Testament that both salvation and redemption are eschatological terms. Something of these, of course, we already have now. But we wait for the day of redemption, the full fruition of God's redeeming, saving act as we enter at the Parousia into the eschatological community of the Messiah. Jesus must come a second time, not to bring the promise of salvation and the first steps of its realization, but the fulfillment of the consummation of the saving grace of God. But here and now we scarce have understood it, and only begun to appropriate it.

One phase of our redemption is the resurrection of our bodies. When Christ comes again the dead in Christ shall be raised. The saints who are yet alive at that time will be instantly changed, Paul told the Thessalonians. In these raised or changed bodies we shall know full redemption. Such complete physical redemption we do not know now, in these bodies which are subject to disease and death. Nor do we yet see the cosmic redemption for which the whole creation groans. The attitude of creation is not a grudged acquiescence to destruction and annihilation, but rather an eager expectation of the time when the earth shall be freed from the prisonhouse of its decay, and share in the glorious freedom of the sons of God (Romans 8:21). This is a part of the process by which a new creation shall displace the old. Certainly it was for some good purpose that the immortal Christ brought this physical universe into being. A new age in a new kind of setting—this is what is intended for the day of Jesus Christ which is yet to come.

Much more will the immortal Christ, the One who is to come, bring us to know in the age to come. He will bestow upon us the eternal inheritance which even now has been promised us in Christ. He will carry out the judgeship which was given Him even in His first coming, but will be finally exercised in the great doomsday when His wrath and His mercy will separate between condemnation and reward. He will bring to its destined perfection the kingdom of God which is in its less perfect stages since Christ first came to earth.

Some Christians fear that the eternity which we are expecting to spend with Christ may become monotonous and tiresome. One person suggested that such a long songfest might be too much!

But the center of eternal interest and occupation will be Christ Himself, the Immortal One whose creative power will be endlessly revealed. He will doubtless lead us in eternal exploration. We may not all start at the same place. For certainly we have not made equal progress in spiritual knowledge and growth. But wherever we start, there will be plenty of range in the university of God for us to search and probe and understand and appreciate.

God has eternal purposes which He will fulfill for us in the Christ who was and is and is to come. May endless praise be His!

John M. Drescher, Scottdale, Pennsylvania, is pastor of the Scottdale Mennonite Church. From 1962 to 1973 he was editor of *Gospel Herald,* the official weekly magazine of the Mennonite Church.

He was pastor of the Crown Hill Mennonite Church, Rittman, Ohio, from 1954 to 1961 and served as bishop/overseer in the Ohio and Eastern Mennonite Conference from 1960 to 1964.

Drescher was assistant moderator of the Mennonite Church in the 1967-69 biennium and moderator during the 1969-71 term.

He received his formal training at Goshen Biblical Seminary (1953-54), Eastern Mennonite College and Seminary (1949-53), and Elizabethtown College (1947-49). He was named Alumnus of the Year by Eastern Mennonite College in 1973.

Drescher has written for approximately 100 magazines and journals, often in the area of family life. He is author of *Meditations for the Newly Married, Now Is the Time to Love, Follow Me, Prayers for All Seasons, Spirit Fruit, Talking It Over,* and *Seven Things Children Need,* as well as of eleven Visitation Pamphlets for ministers, chaplains, and doctors. He has contributed chapters to five additional books.

John and his wife, Betty, are the parents of three boys and two girls: John Ronald, Sandra, Rose, Joseph, and David. The family enjoys music, crafts, camping, clocks, and gardening.